CLIMBING
THE STEPS TO
QINGCHENG
MOUNTAIN

CLIMBING THE STEPS TO QINGCHENG MOUNTAIN

*A Practical Guide
to the Path of Daoist
Meditation and
Qigong*

WANG YUN

SINGING DRAGON
LONDON AND PHILADELPHIA

Disclaimer: The practice of qigong is intended to be a complementary therapeutic practice, its primary goal being prevention of disease through the strengthening of the body's immune and musculoskeletal systems, and the regulation of respiratory and circulatory functions. It is not intended as a replacement for professional and timely medical care. The reader is urged to consult a medical professional on any matter concerning their health, and to follow the given diagnoses and prescriptions.

Harking back to its classical, poetical roots, the Chinese language relies heavily on figures of speech such as hyperbole and metaphors, in order to evoke strong, multisensorial responses in the reader. While rendered in English translation some statements may seem definitive absolutes, they are rather meant to convey the rhetorical strength of a given argument in the original: they are to be taken for their suggestive, evocative power, rather than literally.

First published in 2019
by Jessica Kingsley Publishers
73 Collier Street
London N1 9BE, UK
and
400 Market Street, Suite 400
Philadelphia, PA 19106, USA

www.jkp.com

Copyright © Bhagavan Publishing 2019

Translated by the Modern Wisdom Translation Group

Library of Congress Cataloging in Publication Data
A CIP catalog record for this book is available from the Library of Congress

British Library Cataloguing in Publication Data
A CIP catalogue record for this book is available from the British Library

ISBN 978 1 78775 076 0
eISBN 978 1 78775 077 7

Printed and bound in the United States

我真誠地希望閱
讀本書將有助於
您實現更健康更
幸福的生活

王源

*It is my sincere wish that reading this book will benefit you
on your journey toward realizing a healthier, happier life.*

Wang Yun

CONTENTS

Editor's Preface

It was a time of celebration for the students of Wang Yun when *Climbing the Steps to Qingcheng Mountain* came out in the Chinese language. Indeed, we had long had access to this knowledge and much more in the course of our study with him; yet he had always offered it to us following the traditional way: that is, when the opportunity arose and of course, orally. Emphasis on oral transmission is a common characteristic of traditional knowledge in both the East and the West, but despite its many virtues, the language barrier for foreigners can be a real issue, and all the more so with our woefully faulty memories.

This book fulfilled many of our wishes. It offered a comprehensive overview of the foundations of *qigong* and Daoist meditation, as well as hinting at further developments of these practices. It also offered us some of the lore that surrounds this millenary tradition and its famed immortals, men who remain shrouded in mystery despite their legendary status. More importantly, it offered us a glimpse into the life and apprenticeship of our own teacher, someone who, in many ways, seems to have strode out of these historical mists himself. Indeed, in the same vein as the wily and self-deprecating ancestors of his lineage, catching Wang Yun in the mood to talk about his own story oftentimes feels like catching the trail of a mountain hermit.

Wang Yun is a prolific author, and writes on many topics. He not only traverses the "three peaks" of Daoism, Confucianism and Buddhism, but tethers all of his knowledge to earth with his gentle insistence on grounding all advice and wisdom in daily life. It was no easy task, then, to choose which face of the mountain would appeal to a Western adventurer without hurling them into the clouds.

Wang Yun has said that Daoism, to this day, keeps a special place in his heart. This sentiment is echoed in our team of translators, and we felt greatly enthused at the idea of sharing with our own cultures the lore of immortals and the practical methods for health cultivation they have left to posterity. Also, we share the belief that Daoism's potential contribution to society as a viable form of "medicine," and how it can affect health in everything from diet, to supplements, to exercise, to the mind, has only begun to be explored. In short, we believed that publishing this book in the English language would serve the Daoist teachings that are so dear to us, and as well bring tangible benefits to the reader.

In many ways, this lore is alive and well among us in the form of stories and firsthand accounts of people for whom *qigong* was decisive in assisting their ailments, from the commonplace to the potentially fatal, and granting them a long and healthy life. Wang Yun once recounted the anecdote of an elderly lady he had met while studying with his Daoist master as a youth. Some decades had passed since their last encounter and he one day came across her while walking in the street. Although she was well into her 90s, he described her as having a brisk step, a straight spine, and lively eyes.

The benefits of a regular *qigong* routine are quite numerous. An inexhaustive list includes: better circulation, digestion and immunity; higher and more stable energy levels; the reduction of chronic ailments, bodily pain and old injuries; better sleep quality; a clearer mind; and stabler emotions. A sustained and diligent practice could reap such results as the complete mending of old injuries and the disappearance of any chronic ailment, as well as very high levels of immunity and vitality. Many on our team and our class attendees who started studying with Wang Yun found the regular practice of *qigong* combined with other methods, such as meditation and lifestyle changes, could be a cure for depression, alcohol and drug addiction, short tempers, insomnia, anxiety, and even relationship problems. In our gratitude, we have endeavored to share this treasure of health and vitality we have received by means of certain outreach programs, such as teaching in schools throughout Taiwan, and we now plan to do so with the growing population of the elderly.

The practice of qigong is intended to be a complementary therapeutic practice, its primary goal being prevention of disease through the strengthening of the body's immune and musculoskeletal systems, and the regulation of respiratory and circulatory functions. It is not intended as a replacement from professional and timely medical care. The reader is urged to consult a medical professional on any matter concerning their health, and to follow the given diagnoses and prescriptions.

Harking back to its classical, poetical roots, the Chinese language relies heavily on figures of speech such as hyperbole and metaphors, in order to evoke strong, multisensorial responses in the reader. While rendered in English translation some statements may seem definitive absolutes, they are rather meant to convey the rhetorical strength of a given argument in the original: they are to be taken for their suggestive, evocative power, rather than literally.

But let us come back to Mount Qingcheng, one of China's mythical mountains. From it, generations have sprouted forth to discover, realize, and preserve the recipes that stimulate the deep potential of the human body, beginning with the great Zhang Daoling. As the story goes, he attained immortality and "ascended to the heavens." The title we have chosen for this English translation is a hint at the ascension undertaken by Wang Yun as a young seeker, of the inner journey he took and one he now takes the reader on.

This translation has spanned the course of two years and has been an odyssey of sorts for our team. We feel it necessary to introduce to the reader the wild and vast ocean in which our—and by the same token, your—voyage takes place: the Chinese language. The Chinese language is pictographic and is the culmination of over 5,000 years of transformation from the original ideograms into the 50,000 or so that exist in the most complete dictionaries. The characters are thus the product of history and a scholar could tell fascinating stories about the evolution and multiplicity of meaning within each one. Some are exclusive to a certain context, such as medicine, Buddhism, and of course Daoism. Some characters also take an entirely different meaning when assembled with other characters, and some such grouping of characters can be obscure to even a highly literate native speaker.

The beauty and clarity of Wang Yun's prose in the original Chinese is noteworthy, and similarly, he is a formidably articulate speaker who can meld equally formidable, ancient forms of the Chinese language, and poetry, right into his speech. Most of the time, however, he speaks in a very down-to-earth and practical tone while citing modern writers—both Chinese and foreign—alongside Confucius, Laozi, or the Buddha. It's not hard to imagine that as foreign students of Wang Yun, we can at once be mesmerized and utterly nonplussed at times. In more formal class settings, we will sometimes turn to our Taiwanese counterparts to ask: "What did that mean?" to be answered with an embarrassed "I'm not sure" or a frank "I have no idea." And yet he is also dear to his students for his humor and lightheartedness, always willing to patiently hear out their troubles and offer a new perspective, or intersperse a lecture on Confucian ethics with humorous anecdotes and enchanting stories.

This text was certainly written with the intent to make it accessible to the general public. The challenge in this is evident when we understand that Daoist lore is quite similar to our Western alchemical traditions in that the language is ornate and codified, often to veil the knowledge within so that it remains only accessible to the initiate through transmission from the holder of an authentic lineage. Yet, however strong the desire to simplify may be, the author nonetheless had to remain faithful to the traditions he represents, and there were consequently many technical words and expressions which remained ours to decipher.

Interestingly enough, the Chinese words for "question" and "problem" are one and the same, and a few examples will suffice to illustrate the range of questions we encountered. For a start, one of the most foundational concepts of *qigong* practice is what is known in English as an individual's "essence," "*qi*" (氣), and "spirit." One need only a glance to spot the odd one. The question here was whether or not to translate "*qi*" into English and lose some of its meaning or to leave in its relatively widespread Chinese version. Indeed "*qi*" can be translated as "vital energy," "breath," or even "air." We opted for the Chinese so as to preserve the various levels of meaning this word contains.

Another case we encountered was that of those expressions in which the Chinese characters posed no problem, but their usage was particular to Daoism. This was true for individual characters and expressions. Thus, "汞" (*gong*) or "mercury" represents the "*shen*" (the "spirit") and "採小藥" (*cai xiao yao*) literally means "plucking the little medicine"—a rather cute expression, but not that revealing. In the context of Daoism though, it refers to a very clear stage of the practitioner's inner cultivation, a milestone of sorts. For such cases, we usually let the text explain itself, and explained the term when necessary. Some of the range of meaning might have been lost at times, as is inevitable in any translation, but we have done our utmost to stick to the spirit, rather than the letter, of the word.

This journey was certainly challenging, but also greatly rewarding. The mutual support of our team of translators and the much-appreciated help of Taiwanese students of Wang Yun led to many a joyful breakthrough. As the translated text took shape, we were quite amazed to discover the generosity and thoroughness with which our teacher had imparted crucial concepts and practices for the aspiring *qigong* practitioner and simply curious reader alike. We consider ourselves privileged to have been able to look into the text so closely and see the sequence and larger context of the practice of *qigong*. Indeed, as aspiring practitioners ourselves, this endeavor offered us the opportunity to glean much helpful advice as we perused passages again and again, and not the least of the benefits we received was the time we got to spend with Wang Yun to clarify the terms. With his customary generosity, we at times got more than we'd hoped for: our questions answered and some new ideas to contemplate.

We would now like to invite you to the text itself. The storyline itself flows quite freely, and we suggest that you let yourself be led by its course free of preconception, receptive to the overarching spirit of Daoist practice the author seeks to convey. The individual practices presented therein will thereby make more sense. Due to the subtle nature of the practices, we ourselves have come to realize that in every reading you may glimpse a layer of meaning previously overlooked. This is also due to the fact that as you start practicing the exercises presented herein, your personal experience will deepen your understanding of such abstract concepts as *qi* and the marvelous effects incurred by seemingly simple movements. Moreover, the reader will find a more systemized version of the practices in the Appendix. As *qigong* practice is best conducted under the guidance of a qualified teacher, we welcome you to contact us with any queries that may come up during your practice. With this final note, we will hold you back no more, and see you off on a journey we hope will be one of health, rejuvenation, and many inner discoveries.

Modern Wisdom Translation Group
mwtg.inquiries@gmail.com
January 2019

CHAPTER **1**

UNDER THE BRIGHT SPRING SUN
Meeting My Daoist Master

A sense of warmth and peace is what I remember feeling the first time I stepped through the gates into my Daoist master's residence.

It was a remarkable place, the likes of which I had rarely seen in my 16 or 17 years growing up in Taipei. Even the courtyard left an indelible imprint on my memory. At the main entrance stood two grass-colored sliding iron doors. They were framed by red bricks that had been inlaid with ornately carved wood in the shape of the eight trigrams.[1] Past the gate was a path lined with towering camphor trees and shadowed on one side by a gargantuan banyan tree that stretched its limbs over the roof. Two Japanese mejiro birds sat perched in cages hung from the tree's broad branches.

In the summer, the osmanthus trees encircling the courtyard would sway in the warm breeze and fill the air with their strong perfume. The scent would seep right into your pores and always left me feeling warm and exuberant. At times, I would enjoy a moment near the giant banyan, watching as leaves floated to the ground and the mejiro chirped above.

There was a lawn to one side and, although it wasn't large, 10 to 20 people could sit comfortably and meditate on the grass. A granite staircase rose from the front of the green patch up to an old house that once belonged to the Japanese foreign ministry.

The interior of the house was plain and unadorned. It contained nothing more than bamboo, a tatami mat, and a hardwood floor made of Chinese cypress. Occupying one wall was a wooden sliding door set with rice paper and overlaid with a wooden lattice. I have

---

1   八卦 (*Bagua*). In Daoist cosmology these represent the fundamental principles of reality, seen as a range of eight interrelated concepts.

a deep memory of another door, which stretched the length of the wall and on which was a painting of a flock of cranes. They were captured as they would act in nature: Some were suspended mid-flight, others roosting, others foraging for food.

Three days a week, students from every profession would come to learn how to meditate. I alone was required to arrive early every morning between 4:30am and 5am, rain or shine, to receive the piercing instructions of my *sifu*. Over the years, I saw many people come and go. From all of the fortunate encounters I had with these students, I gathered stories on their personal experiences with meditation and its effects. These would support me as I walked the first leg of my journey into the practice of meditation.

One of my *sifu*'s older students left a deep mark on me. He had a thick Sichuanese accent, was already over 70 years old and had been attending to *sifu* for many years by the time I arrived.

He was very ill when he first moved to Taiwan, as he would recount. He didn't know any doctors and suffered from high blood pressure—systolic over 200—as well as diabetes and obesity. In addition, as a writer and artist with an active imagination, he would wake up constantly throughout the night, if he could sleep at all. The physical and mental torment of his circumstances made his life nearly unbearable.

Sifu had taught him the basics of meditation, with which he gradually started to open acupoints[2] across his body, through a practice known in the Daoist system as *guanqiao*.[3] In time, he was given oral tips[4] for breathing to accompany the work of holding his focus on these various acupoints.

Every day, he would find time to exert himself in his meditation practice, sometimes sitting seven or eight times in a day. He said: "When I first started, I was not able to sit in the full lotus[5] posture. I couldn't even sit in a half-lotus for five minutes. Still, *sifu* said

---

2   穴道 (*xuedao*). Important energy points along the channel system that influence the body if stimulated.

3   關竅 (*guanqiao*). A practice involving the "observation" of the acupoints.

4   竅訣 (*qiaojue*). Pertinent clues given to practitioners at the right time to forward their practice.

5   雙盤 (*shuangpan*). Traditional Indian meditation posture with the feet placed on either thigh.

that it didn't matter. I could simply sit in whatever posture was comfortable and concentrate on the breath."

He continued with his meditation, without stopping, for half a year. By the end, he had lengthened his sessions from five minutes to a whole hour at a time.

He told us about the process: "Within about three months of beginning meditation, my legs wouldn't get cold, numb, or stiff. On the contrary, I would get a warm feeling traveling from the *yongquan*[6] point on the soles of my feet all the way up to my belly, although it wouldn't last for long. From the *dantian*,[7] it would then travel up to my chest and upper back."

"During this time, my appetite increased. I stopped having dreams at night. My blood pressure was reduced by half and, during the day, I didn't get spells of listlessness as I had in the past."

After half a year had passed, he went to the clinic again. The doctor said that his blood sugar levels had almost returned to normal.

---

6   涌泉 (*yongquan*). A major point in *qigong* exercises, it is located on the middle of the sole of the foot, in a soft depression. It is approximately one-third of the distance from the toes to the heel.

7   丹田 (*dantian*). Literally means "red field" or "cinnabar field." It is a focal point for most *qigong* and meditation practices, located approximately 3 finger widths below the navel, inside the lower abdomen.

CHAPTER 2

DAOIST MEDITATION AND HEREDITARY PREDISPOSITION TO ILLNESS

Many people would gather at *sifu*'s residence to learn and seek consultation. During one of these gatherings, a man in his 50s had been sitting off to the side amongst a gregarious group of students. He had been anxiously waiting for a chance to ask a question of one of the senior practitioners. Finally, when the chance arose, he put forth his long-awaited question: "I am genetically predisposed to high blood pressure and diabetes. In addition to this, my work requires me to be quite social, making cigarettes and alcohol a part of the job description. Over the past two years, I seem to have found myself playing this part even more than in the past. I am becoming thinner. I feel tired all day and I am beset with headaches and spells of dizziness. It goes without saying that all this has had an effect on my performance at work. Do you have any advice?"

The senior student, Mr. Duan, was a highly cultured and self-possessed man who tended to all of us with great care. He replied: "Back when I first started studying, the medical system here was not entirely reliable; on more than one occasion, I was given the wrong prescription for lowering my blood pressure, leaving me uncomfortable and feeling like death warmed over.

"I remember during that time a bit of advice *sifu* gave me: 'Meditation requires perseverance—you cannot be inconsistent.

Right now you are deficient in essence, *qi*, and spirit.[8] You must learn to conserve energy and *qi* whenever you exert yourself, and to replenish your energy and vital essence.'

"For this purpose, I was told not to sleep in the same bed as my wife for three months. At that time I had only recently arrived in Taiwan and was newly married to a Taiwanese woman 30 years younger than me! My teacher advised me to take 100 days to restore my lost energy and rebuild my body upon a stronger foundation.

"My master also gave me a few dietary guidelines and prescribed some Chinese medicinal herbs to be picked up at an apothecary. He said that the most important thing for the time being would be to reduce my desire, build up my *qi*, meditate more, and see where this would take me."

Mr. Duan was able to sleep apart from his wife for four months. This allowed him to empty his mind of desires so that even the thought of intimacy did not occur to him. Then his teacher gave him further instructions, which Mr. Duan shared with us.

His *sifu* had told him that it was actually very simple: "All you have to do is practice according to my instructions, whenever you are able. Don't be too concerned with the position of the legs at first. With a soft gaze, focus the eyes on a point about one fist's distance from the nose. Don't even worry about the breath; just relax the body and mind. Don't let the brain run off with any distracting thoughts or concepts. Do this for a week."

Sifu continued by telling him to take some time to relax the whole body from head to toe before sitting to meditate. This meant relaxing every hair on the body, and even the bones, blood, the five organs and six viscera,[9] and every cell. He was to accompany this with the breath but without paying particular attention to it.

---

8   精氣神 (*jing qi shen*). The aim of the Daoist is to transform essence to *qi* and finally to spirit. Essence (*jing*) is tied to the essential *qi* of the kidneys and used in the reproductive system: from the essence, stored in the viscera and used in the reproductive system, one's energy moves. The Chinese concept of spirit (*shen*) is what normally makes us conscious and awake during the day; it's also the ability to interact with people and be aware of our surrounding environment. The interplay of the three is a process carefully regulated by the able practitioner in order to transform *jing* to *qi* and *qi* to *shen*.

9   五臟六腑 (*wu zang liu fu*). According to Chinese Medicine, the internal body is composed of five organs and six viscera. The five organs refer to the *yin* "organs," while the six viscera refer to the *yang* "organs" of the internal body.

It went on like this for another week. The strange thing was that Mr. Duan's blood pressure dropped, quite perceptibly, after following the prescribed methods. In the evening he could fall asleep easily and rest without getting up during the night.

CHAPTER 3

THE INTERDEPENDENCE OF THE MIND AND BREATH

Mr. Duan said: "After a month my teacher came to me with more instructions. He said: 'All of the methods I am teaching you are based on the Daoist practices of Patriarch Lu Chunyang.[10] When you sit for meditation, you need only to expel all distracting thoughts and desires, and purify your mind. Your mind and breath will eventually join seamlessly and you will come to feel light and full of energy and vitality. If you can sustain these practices, it will have the effect of naturally regulating and balancing the organs and viscera. These techniques also conform to the principles explained in the *Yellow Emperor's Internal Classic*.[11] They are particularly apt when dealing with chronic problems related to the blood vessels connected to the heart. If you are able to temporarily stop all frivolous, distracting and delusive thoughts and relax the body and mind, the heart will be better able to regulate and aid the functions of the other organs. Furthermore, your blood will circulate more freely and your spirit will be tranquil. Supplement this by reducing your consumption of red meat, refined and oily foods, and sweets, and by adding more boiled greens, and with time your health will turn around.'"

10　呂純陽 Also known as Lu Dongbin (呂洞賓), a Tang Dynasty Chinese scholar and poet who has been elevated to the status of an immortal in the Chinese cultural sphere. He is worshipped especially by the Daoists.

11　黃帝內經 (*Huangdi Neijing*). An ancient Chinese medical text regarded as the fundamental doctrinal source for Chinese Medicine for more than two millennia. Composed of two texts, each of 81 chapters, or treatises, in a question and answer format between the mythical Yellow Emperor and six of his ministers.

CHAPTER 4

A UNIQUE STYLE OF MEDITATION

Unlocking the Brain's Hidden Potential

On a typical day everyone would gather in *sifu's* reception area. It was a rectangular space, about the size of 20 tatami mats, and tucked away in the corner of the room with a long table. Some students would steep and serve tea while everyone listened to Mr. Duan speak about his long years of experience studying under *sifu*.

Mr. Duan continued: "As well as *sifu* being a scholar himself, the practice of Traditional Chinese Medicine in his family runs deep. They have been serving their hometown through five generations of doctors known for their medical gifts. Growing up in this environment, *sifu* picked up things such as acupuncture, knowledge of the channels,[12] muscle and tendon correction and alignment, and the ability to make his own ointments and pills. On top of this, he became skilled in such martial arts as Chinese boxing, the sword, and the staff. As such, his instruction is derived from not just one school of meditation, but from a fusion of various forms of Traditional Chinese Medicine, nutrition, *qi* cultivation,[13] ancient Daoist *qigong*, breathing techniques, and teaching methodology. In this, his treatments are uniquely potent."

Only after a month had gone by, said Mr. Duan, did *sifu* even begin teaching him the cross-legged sitting-meditation technique, as well as explain the meaning and principles behind it. He additionally gave Mr. Duan oral tips concerning the breath. *Sifu* told him one day: "Whenever your body feels heavy and weak or you feel dispirited, place your focus on the air you take in through

---

12　筋經絡 (*jinjingluo*). Routes in the body along which *qi* flows.

13　養身 (*yangshen*). Cultivation techniques that are aimed at increasing or preserving the *qi* of the body.

your in-breaths. Whenever you feel overstimulated, or that your mind is buzzing with scattered thoughts, or you feel like a heat wave is moving through your body, focus on the air as it is expelled through your out-breaths. Count your breaths in this way, upward from 1 to 10 and back down from 10 to 1.

"While counting the breath, try to put all of your concentration on your inhalations and exhalations. Do not, by any means, try to stop, cut off or repress your delusive thoughts.[14] Allow everything to be free and natural, or else you will only cause your *qi* to rise. If you're lucky, over time you can reach a single-minded, pure state which is empty of scattered thoughts. But don't wait in hope and anticipation of this happening."

Cardiovascular problems had been a major concern for Mr. Duan. He would keep himself informed by routinely reading whatever medical literature he could find on the subject. He once told us: "During meditation, as the body and mind become calm and the breath becomes smooth, our cerebral cortex relaxes. The frequency and curve of our brain waves change, depending on the length of the meditator's experience. This in turn affects the frontal lobe and hypothalamus, greatly enhancing the function of the central and sympathetic nervous systems. Once I knew this, it became obvious to me why I no longer needed medication to regulate my blood pressure and why my heart had regained its normal function. My blood vessels had relaxed and expanded, reducing the heart's demand for oxygen, increasing antioxidants in the bloodstream and boosting the circulation of blood through the heart. I saw a considerable surge in my levels of creativity and the quality of my writing, all of which I attributed to meditation. Meditation unlocks the brain's latent potential through the enhanced coordination of its left and right sides. Needless to say, the effects of improved blood flow on all the other organs, the endocrine system and the overall functioning of my metabolism were almost unbelievable."

---

14 雜念 (*zanian*). Thoughts that arise from conditioned emotions and thought patterns, and which keep us in a state of confusion or lack of clarity about the true nature of reality.

CHAPTER 5

COUPLING MEDITATION WITH THE BREATH

Mr. Duan continued: "After a year went by in my meditation practice, *sifu* observed that my breath had become even and fine. I no longer involuntarily alternated between long and short breaths or sporadically cut off in the middle of one. At this point, he gave me further instruction: 'On the in-breath, gently curl the tongue upward toward the upper palate; on the out-breath, curl the tongue downward until it rests on the lower palate.' Although it depends on your physical condition, the exercise should be relatively short and should stop after saliva has filled your mouth."

Mr. Duan then said: "Once saliva has filled your entire mouth, swish it around using your tongue. Once you've done that a number of times, separate the saliva into three parts. Swallow each part individually, guiding it down to the *dantian* with the power of your intention.

"*Sifu* said that the saliva you produce once you enter a state of stillness is very different from that which you normally produce. The enzymes it contains greatly enhance digestion. Furthermore, the breath in this state slowly becomes more refined and prolonged, until at some point it sinks deep into the *dantian*. *Sifu* told me that I had to continue training myself in this key phase of the practice for a while."

After having practiced according to *sifu*'s instructions for three months, one day Mr. Duan felt a wave of warm *qi* ascend from his *yongquan* point up to the area around the *dantian*. It then moved from his lower back to his kidneys and slowly rose upward. It was unlike anything he had experienced before and unnerved him more than a little.

He sought out *sifu*'s advice on what had happened. *Sifu* assured him that it was just a natural result of the practice and that he did not need to dwell on it. He should instead try to maintain a sense of emptiness, silence, stillness, and discernment of the truth of his experiences, foregoing the excessive labeling of physical sensations. What he did need to be on the alert for, however, was a potential surge in his sexual drive. This happens to some people, *sifu* said, as they go through the slow process of physical rehabilitation, something which Mr. Duan was undergoing himself. For some men this will cause morning erections or more frequent intense sexual urges. At this point, it is very important to keep yourself on a tight leash, lest you throw out all of your effort in a moment of recklessness. *Sifu* told him that to quell your desires, focus your attention on a transparent, formless, intangible sphere at the tip of your nose, and they will gradually recede.

CHAPTER **6**

THE RELATION BETWEEN DESIRE
AND THE MOVEMENT OF *QI*

"'Our forefathers all taught us to stop our thoughts, but if thoughts are unceasing, it is to no avail,'" said Mr. Duan, quoting *sifu*. "This is something *sifu* told me when I was first starting out in the practice of meditation," he said. "Many people struggle to grasp this point, because stopping or controlling scattered thoughts is as difficult as trying to stop a torrent of water that has fallen 1,000 meters over a cliff's edge. If you persist in this method, it may become an obsession, which in itself becomes an illness. This is not something the average person can do, nor is it something that you can force your mind to do, unless you have trained to the point where you have restored your lost *yang* energy and essence to a state of youthful vigor. This point, however, belongs to the realm of the mind, and not of the body, so for a very long time I was most distressed in my attempts to grasp it."

Mr. Duan continued: "*Sifu* then said: 'Let everything be natural; forego all clinging; let go of all your connections to this world; leave only the original breath.'[15] Only by going through a period of intense and strenuous spiritual investigation was I able to understand that 'the original breath' is none other than the mind. At that time, I went to *sifu* to confirm this. He said: 'Like a blind cat stumbling by chance upon a dead mouse, you have not struck the mark; but neither are you far off. Apply yourself to your thoughts as a tuner would to the strings of a *guqin*!'[16]

"Sifu continued: 'When you are young, the exercises that come with the first steps of training are in fact very easy: You meditate,

---

15 先天一炁 (*xiantianyiqi*). Can also be translated as "primordial energy."
16 古琴 (*guqin*). Traditional Chinese stringed instrument.

count your breath, sit cross-legged, breathe and focus on points in the body.[17] There is no great challenge there. The challenge starts when your *qi* starts to build and flourish. When you enter into stillness during meditation, your body will very easily start shaking, usually as a result of desire. Many mistakenly believe this to be the restoration of the *yang* energy, and nine out of ten people fall into this trap. 'During this phase, men might experience wet dreams, or perhaps even become accustomed to them. This is very dangerous. There are also some who regard the opening up of the acupoints as a simple matter. *Qi* can go through [these points] in an actual or imaginary way, and for most beginners it indeed does go through, but in an incorrect way. If you do not have an experienced teacher to guide you through the process of opening these points, it can easily cause illness. This is something that should in no way be taken lightly.'"

These words that *sifu* shared really made sense, and can be encapsulated in the idea of being "natural in learning." The main point for grasping these instructions is in the subtle space that lies between using and not using one's intention.

---

17 守竅 (*shouqiao*). The practice of placing one's concentration on various *guanqiao*, or points on the body connected to the Daoist system of channels and acupoints.

CHAPTER 7

MEDITATION TECHNIQUES FOR BETTER SLEEP

There was a student, about 30 or 40 years old, who had been studying sitting meditation for over three years and had been dealing with problems in his practice. For advice, he sought out Mr. Duan and told him about the situation: "I work in sales. As manager of the department, I am responsible for meeting targets and supervising the team. I'm not sure if it's stress from the position, but lately I've had trouble sleeping. When I sit for meditation, I feel especially unfocused and unable to settle my mind. I can feel my heart pounding and my breath gets stuck in my chest. I don't think I'm getting much out of it, and as someone who also practices, I wanted to hear your advice on how to work through this kind of problem."

"Your situation is quite common," Mr. Duan said. "There are numerous reasons for losing sleep. It's known in Traditional Chinese Medicine (TCM) as 'insomnia.' The elderly, those who overuse the brain, those who suffer from excessive phlegm in the bronchi, or those who are physically drained, agitated, and quick to anger are more likely to experience poor sleep quality. In your case, over-thinking has given you poor circulation and is drawing blood to your brain. This, in turn, makes you deficient in *qi* and agitates your mind. In TCM, this is what happens when your body's water and fire elements are imbalanced. You need first and foremost to find an experienced TCM doctor who can help you restore harmony and promote your body's water and fire cycle.[18]

18 水火既濟 (*shuihuojiji*). According to Traditional Chinese Medicine, the five elements in the universe—wind, fire, water, metal, and wood—refer to, and are contained in, different organ systems in the body. When the elements are in harmony and balance, the body is healthy; on the other hand, an excess or deficiency of one or more elements causes imbalance and disease.

In advanced level meditation, there is an oral tip which states 'The mind ends in the spine,'[19] which refers to this method."

Mr. Duan himself had previously suffered from chronic sleep deprivation. He had picked up quite a bit of knowledge on medicine from his Daoist master over his ten years of study, and would often take people's pulses[20] and diagnose other students. A few years ago, he actually became a licensed TCM doctor, illustrating how chronic illness makes a good doctor.

Mr. Duan went on further to explain other causes of sleeplessness, such as poor digestion. Impaired digestion can impact sleep quality or cause one to repeatedly get up throughout the night. This unusual connection highlights the importance of correct diagnosis in prescribing the right medicine.

Mr. Duan later gave another student, surnamed Wu, some recommendations: "An hour before going to bed, put all matters of business to the back of your mind. Listen to some relaxing music. Watch an entertaining television show. Do some light reading. You can soak your feet in a basin of hot salt water for about 15–30 minutes, which helps draw blood downward into your feet. After soaking, use your fingers to massage, or your fist to gently pat, the spot in the middle of your heel. This should be done gently and without causing discomfort."

When he finished speaking, Mr. Duan found that many of those nearby had been listening attentively to their conversation. The student to whom he had given the advice, Mr. Wu, had taken notes furiously without missing a word. This was a quiet moment of inspiration and affirmation for Mr. Duan.

He continued: "In the past, when sound sleep was an elusive dream, my *sifu* taught me a set of techniques from the School of

---

19 心念止於背脊中 (*xinnianzhiyubeijizhong*). Translates literally as "thoughts end in the middle of the back of the spine."

20 把脈 (*bamai*) "pulse diagnosis." In Chinese Medicine the pulse is a very important means to determine illness in the body. In modern times, the pulse is taken at the radial artery on both hands. On each hand, there are three positions (termed the *cun*, *guan*, and *chi* positions). Each position refers to different organ systems of the body, and the pulses vary from the right to the left hand. Furthermore, each pulse position has three levels (depths): superficial, middle, and deep. Through the taking of the pulse, a good doctor can determine very specifically the location of illnesses in the body.

Complete Reality[21] to use while lying down. There is one technique in particular that I consider quite beneficial for people today, and I would like to share it with you.

"It is both simple and easy to carry out. Before sleep, you must remember to rest your mind before closing your eyes. Your breath should be calm and even; your hands should rest naturally at your sides; your legs should lie straight and your toes should be pointing up toward the sky. Breathe through your nostrils. When you exhale, move your toes forward toward the ground. When you inhale, bring your toes back to their resting position. If your mind and body are relaxed and you just follow your breath with the movements, sleep will come naturally."

Mr. Duan added: "This technique has been very effective for me. Within a few moments I am fast asleep, and I sleep very well. In the morning, my wife often complains about how my snoring kept her up all night!"

---

21 全真派 (quanzhenpai). The Quanzhen School of Daoism originated in Northern China. With strong Daoist roots, the Quanzhen School specializes in the process of "alchemy within the body" or neidan (internal alchemy), as opposed to waidan (external alchemy, which experiments with the ingestion of herbs and minerals, etc.).

CHAPTER **8**

A POSTING STANCE
FOR THE OFFICE

Mr. Duan said: "*Sifu* actually taught me more than a few posting[22] stances. There is one that is particularly beneficial for those with desk jobs or who have to sit for a prolonged period of time. Getting up and doing this stance for a bit every hour can help enhance blood circulation. This prevents blood from collecting in the upper part of the body, especially the brain."

Lee, another one of the students listening, and a rather impetuous one at that, jumped in and asked: "Mr. Duan, could you please demonstrate it for us?" Mr. Duan agreed and rose to his feet. He instructed those in attendance to stand with their legs shoulder-width apart. He remained standing until his body had completely relaxed. Then he naturally let his body sink until his legs bent at an angle of 15 degrees. He raised his hands effortlessly to the level of his chest, keeping his fingers slightly separated, with the tips pointing toward each other and about a fist's width apart. With his palms facing inward, he held this posture, with his eyes fixed on a point in front of him.

"In the beginning, breathe naturally," he said. "When the entire body is completely relaxed, begin counting your breath from 1 to 10, then from 10 back to 1. Those with high blood pressure can, after their body has completely relaxed, bring their focus to the *yongquan* point. Doing so draws the blood downward, lowering blood pressure over time. Those with a weak stomach or intestines can, again after becoming physically relaxed, utilize a particular technique for inhalation and exhalation. This involves sucking the

---

22 站椿 (*zhanzhuang*). A particular set of *qigong* methods. In all of these, the body
    remains static and in a set position, much like a post.

belly inward on the in-breath, as if you were trying to bring the breath all the way to the back. On the out-breath, relax and let the belly naturally push forward. Repeat the sequence a couple of times until you feel comfortable. This will aid bowel movement and relieve constipation.

"All in all, there are various techniques for posting. Every individual can benefit from the practice by finding the one best suited to their particular physical condition."

CHAPTER **9**

SUPPLEMENTING YOUR EXERCISE WITH *QI PIAN QUAN SHEN*

After Mr. Duan explained these steps, he told us: "The effect of whichever routine you choose will become more pronounced if you conclude it with the *qi pian quan shen*[23] exercise."

A new student, who worked as a civil servant, replied: "We didn't know about the posting techniques until you taught us just now. Would you mind guiding us through this concluding exercise as well?"

Kindly, and with great attention to detail, Mr. Duan began to explain and demonstrate the exercise to us. He said: "As I mentioned earlier, conclude every *qigong* session with this exercise. Start in the same fashion as the posting exercise by keeping your feet shoulder-width apart. Raise your arms up along the torso with your palms facing up. Once you reach the level of the chest, turn your palms down. Let your body sink down into a squat while your hands sink to the level of the hips. At the bottom of the crouch, extend your arms forward while rising to a full standing position. Once your legs have fully extended, your arms should continue to move upward until they reach over your head. Then let them drop slowly down and stop in front of your lower abdomen at the level of the *dantian*. They should be positioned as if you were holding a ball on its sides. Next, without moving anything from the hips down, gently turn your upper body to the left, then back to the center. Turning to the right, repeat the same movement. Finally, slowly lift your left leg and extend it out and slightly to the side in a kicking motion. Then do the same with

---

23 氣遍全身. A *qigong* practice from the category of "concluding exercises," meant to balance and circulate the *qi* throughout the body at the end of a practice session.

your right leg. When all of this is done, you can let your arms fall naturally to their resting position to complete a whole sequence of *qi pian quan shen*."

Chapter **10**

A Little Secret to Brighten up Your Life

Being younger than my fellow students, over the years I met all manner of people at *sifu*'s residence. Some came after their medical treatments proved to be ineffective; some sought to answer the questions of life through meditation; others were attracted simply by *sifu*'s reputation. The common thread that tied us together was our desire to extend our lives, strengthen our bodies and minds, and gain wisdom from *sifu*'s teachings.

In a display of honesty and affection, *sifu* once said to me: "In my pursuit of the Dao[24] and the Truth, in search of that elusive immortality, I have trod a perilous path, the hardships of which few could comprehend. Over this journey, I have come to the conclusion that spiritual practice and meditation are entirely one's own responsibility: Whatever you come to realize is yours alone, and your spirit is hidden to everyone but yourself. Others could not help you even if they wanted. Our transient life is here and then gone, a shooting star that flashes across the night sky. Whether that star burns hot and bright depends on how early you can discover the secrets of life and death. There must have been some karmic connection[25] at work for someone as young as you to have found the path to longevity.

"There is no shortage these days of people wanting to learn *qigong* practices and develop supernatural abilities. This is actually

---

24 求道 (*qiudao*). The "pursuit of the *Dao*" refers to the study and practice of Daoism. The Dao is typically translated as the "Way," referring to the way of the universe and its laws.

25 緣份 (*yuanfen*). Prevalent in ethnic Chinese cultures, it is the notion that an individual's circumstance is determined by a preconditioned bond or connection that has been built over more than just a single lifetime.

a very dangerous thing. There are also many who believe that sitting meditation can open their conception and governing vessels,[26] and in so doing uncover a knowledge of all things. These wild fantasies are based on misinterpretations of the underlying principles of meditation. Back when I was just a beginner, we were all required to first understand the reasons for practicing meditation. The first to guide me in these studies was a Daoist priest from the School of Complete Reality."

---

26 任督二脈 (renduermai). Two energy channels in the body that play a primary role in *qigong* practice. The conception channel runs through the center of the front, ventral portion of the body. The governing channel runs through the center of the back, dorsal portion of the body.

CHAPTER 11

STEPPING INTO THE WORLD OF ANCIENT CHINESE DAOISM

Sifu spoke of many of his personal experiences in pursuit of the Dao and meditation, a pursuit which began in his childhood. He taught me that the modern conception of Dao is a far cry from what it was in the past. Daoism's vast scope ranges from the thought of Laozi[27] to Daoist rituals such as the use of talismans, as well as the Daoist belief of the harmony of *yin, yang*[28] and the five elements. Throughout China's history, Buddhism and Daoism have mingled closely. Since both schools have continued to be passed on through the generations, their influence can be found in every Chinese dynastic era. The number of Daoist doctrines and schools of thought is staggering. Each has its own views and interpretations, making it tricky to find a consensus among them.

In his compilations, Liu Xie[29] of the Liang dynasty attempted to categorize Daoist scholars into three subdivisions. He credited the lineage that began with Laozi and ran through to Zhang Daoling[30] as authentic on account of the consistency with which they wrote on the Dao, the emphasis in their works on the principle of non-

---

27 老子. Ancient Chinese philosopher and writer, reputed author of the *Tao Te Ching* (the main text of Daoism), founder of philosophical Daoism, and a deity in religious Daoism and traditional Chinese religions.

28 陰陽. From a Daoist perspective, or classical Chinese perspective, everything that exists in the material world can be classified into *yin* and *yang*. *Yin* refers to passive elements while *yang* refers to active elements.

29 劉勰. Chinese writer, author of China's greatest work of literary aesthetics, *The Literary Mind and the Carving of Dragons*. His biography is included in the *Liangshu*.

30 張道陵. Eastern Han Dynasty Daoist figure credited with founding a Daoist sect called the "Way of the Celestial Masters." Sometimes pictured riding on a tiger, one of the "Four Celestial Masters."

action,[31] and their singular focus on the same principles. He particularly praised their focus on the practice of the *Li Zong*,[32] and the fact that all the writings of the lineage accord with its spiritual practices. Liu Xie deemed other schools wrapped up in immortality, supernatural phenomena, pills, longevity through sexual practices, or the elimination of evil forces, as divergent sects.

Other writers divided Daoist practices into internal and external methods. All of the Daoist literature, biographies, and scriptures were considered "internal," whereas precepts, supplementary medicine, "bedroom arts" (Daoist sexual practices), talismans, and similar practices were considered "external." Owing to their mixed and multifaceted nature, Confucian scholars eventually grouped all Daoist schools into sects according to the specific practices each pursued. There was the Qingjing Sect,[33] those which practiced *fulu*,[34] the sects which focused on the transformation of primordial *jing* into *qi*, and those which made use of rare Chinese Medicine. Those who try to pursue these practices without having correct views or understanding of these matters, however, could easily go astray, resulting in harm to both themselves and others. Among such examples in history are Li Shaojun (2nd century BCE), Yu Ji (2nd century CE), Zhang Jiao (2nd century CE), and Zhao Guizhen (9th century CE).

Sifu said: "I was lucky as a boy because I had frequent chances to visit Buddhist and Daoist temples in the Qingcheng[35] area, which afforded me acquaintance with a number of Buddhist and Daoist masters as well as adept practitioners. When my learning first started, my *sifu* didn't teach me any Daoist rituals, talismans, writing, or mantras; he simply told me to read the Daoist scriptures from the temple collection whenever I had free time. For the following six or seven years, I would spend most of my time perusing texts on Daoist alchemy written throughout the various

---

31 無為 (*wuwei*). Laozi explains that beings (or phenomena) that are wholly in harmony with the Dao behave in a completely natural, uncontrived way. This is the goal of spiritual practice, according to Laozi: the attainment of this purely natural way of behaving; effortless and spontaneous movement.

32 理宗. One of the four divisions of Daoist practice.

33 清淨派. This was one of the branches of the Complete Reality School.

34 符籙. A form of exorcism that involves writing supernatural talismans.

35 青城. In *Sichuan* province, China.

dynasties. Whenever I encountered things I didn't understand, I would consult the many tremendously helpful Daoist teachers at the temple. I was blessed to have immersed myself over and over again in the writings of such Daoist schools and thinkers as Huang Di (the famed Yellow Emperor), Laozi, Zhuangzi (4th century CE), Liezi (4th century BCE), Chi Songzi (1st century CE), Wei Boyang (2nd century CE), Lu Qianxu (16th century CE), and Zhu Yunyang (mid 17th century). This doesn't include the hundreds of other rare and valuable Daoist collections of writings I found. Among them, the *Marrow of the Crimson Phoenix* from the Ming dynasty (1368–1644 CE) contains certain oral tips that were inaccessible to Daoist practitioners of the Tang (618–906 CE), Song (960–1279 CE), and Yuan (1279–1368 CE) dynasties. In light of all of this, I could not help but feel in awe at the magnificent richness of Daoism.

What really got my blood pumping back then was getting my hands on the secret texts of Fu Qingzhu (1607–1684 CE). He was one of six great Qing dynasty masters I admired the most in my youth—the others being Gu Yanwu (1613–1682 CE), Huang Zongxi (610–1695 CE), Wang Fuzhi (1619–1692 CE), Li Yong (1627–1705 CE), and Yan Yuanyi (1635–1704 CE). Fu Qingzhu's poetry, essays, calligraphy, medical expertise, stone engraving, and *kung fu*, as well as his moral character and scholarly attainments, have been greatly admired and followed through the ages. The famous Fugong Temple in Taiyuan[36] was built in his honor.

I am especially partial, having always been fond of calligraphy, to Master Fu's book on the subject, in particular his views on the principles of the art form. He advocated a style that is simple and unadorned over fine and delicate, rustic and unpolished over rosy and gaudy.

Owing to his family traditions, Fu had distinctive views on the subject of health cultivation.[37] He proposed the regular use of *huang jing*,[38] attributing his youthful energy to his regular intake of the herb from a young age."

---

36 太原. Capital of Shanxi province, China.
37 養生 (*yangsheng*). Health cultivation techniques, to prolong life, that have developed in China throughout its long history.
38 黃精. Solomon's seal, a genus of flowering plants.

CHAPTER 12

A BOOKWORM AMONG THE LIBRARIES OF DAOIST MEDITATION CLASSICS

Sifu continued: "Fu Qingzhu shared the magnetic personality of his peer, Meng Changjun (d. 279 BCE). Fu's chivalrous and amiable nature attracted the friendship of talented, wise, and intelligent people from all walks of life, and it also facilitated his impact on every level of society. Nobles and high officials would scramble to add his arguments, writings, poems, essays, and paintings to their collections. His reputation even earned him the jealous hatred of those in power.

"Such a legend was this figure from the Qing dynasty, that his life would fuel the pages of stories for generations to come. When I first got my hands on the books *Master Danting's Secret Book of Daoism*—compiled by Fu himself—and *The Daoist Guide of Inner Practice* by Hua Tuo (140–208 BCE), I was brought to the brink of tears with excitement and emotion. Any chance I got, I would transcribe and memorize them. Whenever I came upon the books' many profound and inscrutable passages, I would seek the advice of *sifu* in private. This would later prove helpful when reading the *Yellow Court Classic*.

"I could say of some of the others I read at the time—notably *A Great Compilation of Daoism*, *The Secret Book of Daoist Enlightenment*, *The Secret Book of the Great Path*, and *A Compendium of the Daoist Canon*—that if you were to search for 1,000 years, you might not find anything resembling them. Buried in these books, I would think to myself that, were I to become a bookworm living on the words of these Daoist masters and practitioners who had sought the truth, I would do so without the least regret."

Despite my young age and the pressures of schoolwork, my meditation and *qigong* studies with *sifu* continued entirely in secret. Not even my parents knew. I could only rely on my memory of *sifu*'s lessons and the bits and pieces I managed to jot down after my visits. Thinking back, I regret not being able to remember more. It was as if I had returned empty-handed from an island of treasures. It pains me to think back on it.

Strictly speaking, the myriad philosophies from different scholars in China remained fragmented until the Zhou dynasty (1046–221 BCE). It was not until Confucius created his own philosophy that the distinction between Confucianism and Daoism became apparent.

Emperor Wu (156–87 BCE), the seventh emperor of the Han dynasty, followed Dong Zhongshu's[39] suggestion of making Confucianism the official ethical system of China. Daoist *sutras* were confined to the forgotten rows of bookshelves for a time. When the Northern and Southern dynasties later emerged, so too did Neo-Daoism (3rd to 6th century CE) and the Seven Sages of the Bamboo Grove.[40] Studies of Laozi and Zhuangzi again came into vogue, and Daoism flourished for a long stretch of history.

Daoism's origins can be traced as far back as Fuxi (2852–2738 BCE) and Shen Nong (c. 2000 BCE). The religion was officially sanctioned by the Yellow Emperor and its various divisions were unified by Li Er (c. 500 BCE). In time, philosophers began to regard Daoism as mainstream, and drew from it to develop their own thought. For example, Zhuangzi, Liezi, and Shang Yang (390–338 BCE) all used it to formulate their views on political reform. Later came the publication of *Gui Gu Zi*[41] as well as two important figures in Daoism's development: Yi Yin (1648–1549 BCE), a minister in the early Shang dynasty, and Huang Shigong (3rd century CE, also known as Xia Huanggong), who taught the Han dynasty the art of

---

39 董仲舒. An influential philosopher, established Confucianism in the Han Dynasty (179–104 BCE).

40 竹林七賢 (*zhu lin qi xian*). A group of Chinese scholars, writers, and musicians of the 3rd century CE.

41 鬼谷子. One of the founders of The School of Diplomacy in the Warring States era. A renowned philosopher, diplomat, prophet, and educator.

war. Daoism formed the backbone of all of these figures and their philosophies.

In the generations to come, noted figures such as Ge Hong (283 CE), Wei Boyang,[42] and Qiu Chuji (1148–1227) would all fall under what would become known as the School of *Dan Ding*.[43] Astrology, divination, numerology, and other mysterious and bizarre pseudo-spiritual pursuits would all fall under the Daoist ethos. Even the realm of supernatural beings would become consolidated under Daoism. Another way to explain these "internal" and "external" schools and their principles is as products of the various folk cultures that developed throughout Chinese history. But they cannot escape their orbit around the larger mass of Chinese Daoism.

---

42   魏伯陽. A noted Chinese author and alchemist of the Eastern Han Dynasty.

43   丹鼎派. *Dan* is the immortal pill produced through Daoist alchemy. *Ding* is the vessel in which it is contained.

Chapter 13

Skill in Meditation: It's All About the Mind

The gradual progress of my training under my Daoist master did not stop with the basic practices of sitting meditation and *qigong*. His instructions centered on cultivating the quality of a practitioner's moral character and mind.

He said: "Within the *Yi Jing*,[44] it says 'Inquire after ultimate truth and bring out the best of a person's self-nature, to the end that both are integrated into a person's life.' Reaching the 'oneness of heaven and humanity' during meditation, however, depends entirely on the training and disciplining of the mind.

"If you sit there like a stagnant pool of water, you will definitely miss the true power of meditation, and it will be of no benefit whatsoever to your health. While you are still young, you should use that good head of yours to memorize a few books I have for you, front to back. Ask any questions that come to mind while you read them. Ask often. You may not yet have discovered the wonders inside these pages, but once you reach a higher level in your meditation practice, you will feel yourself reaching a deeper understanding of them."

Sifu was in the habit of closing his eyes in contemplation; his expression is one that still remains vivid in my mind.

He continued: "During my years on Qingcheng Mountain, my Daoist master specially assigned a few books for me to read. One of these was Wei Boyang's *The Kinship of the Three*.[45] That's why I've wanted you to memorize and become well versed in the *Yi Jing* and its divinatory symbols. This was all in the hope that you would

---

44 易經. *Book of Changes*, an ancient Chinese divination text and the oldest Chinese classic.

45 參同契 *(Can Tong Qi)*. Second-century book on Daoist alchemy.

have fewer obstructions when it came time to read *The Kinship of the Three*. The three volumes under this title are all based on the trigrams found in the *Yi Jing*.

"In actual fact, what it does is expose very thoroughly, by means of the trigrams, the innate essence of the *Dan Jing*.[46] Consequently, any connoisseur or expert in the field will be familiar with it, and so you must also read more. Also make sure that you don't read the *Book of the Master Who Embraces Simplicity* as you would read a novel. It contains some parts that discuss secret and mysterious things. However, the main point is to help you better understand the universe, heaven, and earth, the microcosm of our human body, the process through which the ancients manufactured the golden pill,[47] and the process of practicing and actualizing the path of the immortals.

"Also spend more time with the sections covering the cultivation of vitality. You need not linger too long on the parts dealing with political thought. Right now, you are at the level of 'cultivating *qi*' in preparation for future practices; there is still much knowledge left for you to commit to memory. Whenever you have spare time in the mornings and evenings, you should also recite the *Scripture of Purity and Quiescence*[48] so as to refine your temperament."

---

46 丹經 A generic term which refers to canonic texts of Daoist internal alchemy.

47 丹藥 (*dan yao*). An elixir or pill sought by Chinese alchemists to confer physical or spiritual immortality. There are both internal and external methods used to achieve such a pill.

48 清靜經 (*Qing Jing Jing*). An anonymous Tang Dynasty Daoist classic on the elimination of desire in order to cultivate spiritual purity and stillness.

CHAPTER 14

WATER FROM AN EMPTY CUP

"For the mind to be still, one must see through fame, riches, honor, and romance," *sifu* continued. "In the process of meditating, many people use their intention in an attempt to control their discursive thoughts. This is like trying to put out a fire by pouring oil on the logs: It confuses the cause for the effect. You can't just use force or sheer willpower to tell your mind to stop thinking. Its transformation must start from the very root: desire and attachment.

"Have you ever noticed that when you are not meditating your mind is free of distracted thought? Yet whenever you want to sit and become still you feel as if your head is suddenly filled with the relentless stampede of 1,000 galloping horses. The principle behind this is akin to shaking a glass of water and setting it on a table in the sun. You would be able to see many little objects floating about. This is what happens when we meditate. If you want to make your mind tranquil, you have to empty the glass. When you want to become still during meditation, first you must empty the mind. If the mind is scattered, the spirit will be muddled. If the mind is empty, the spirit will be clear. If the mind is occupied, desires will be many. If the mind is unoccupied, it will be clear and empty.

"If you want to meditate, you should therefore first empty your mind and clear away desire. You can try reciting the *Heart Sutra* one to three times before starting your session. The *Heart Sutra* is an essential text in both the Buddhist and Daoist traditions. As the School of Complete Reality [to which *sifu* belonged] does not distinguish between Buddhist and Daoist practices—a fact which makes our school unique among the branches of Daoism—it would be appropriate for you to learn and go deeper into the *Heart Sutra*. Its meaning is especially profound and unfathomable."

CHAPTER 15

GETTING PREPARED
FOR MEDITATION

Sifu said: "You can regularly make use of the method I just taught you, known as the 'Six Word Secret,'[49] to remove toxic *qi* from your five viscera and six bowels. During meditation, you must also be sure to properly adjust and balance the body, from the four limbs to the bones and channels. This is a simple, quick way to prevent impure *qi* from getting stuck in the body.

"Before meditating, first stretch out your arms and legs, massage your joints and acupoints, rotate your head and your eyes around in their sockets, tuck the chin in slightly and bring the head back a number of times. Then move the head to the left and right toward the shoulders. Finally, rotate the head and neck clockwise and counterclockwise a few times.

"Following this, rotate the shoulders and arms by swinging the arms from left to right. Next, bring the hands together and bend forward at the waist as you try and touch the ground. Third, place the hands on the hips and twist the torso to the left and to the right. Fourth, make full circles with your hips. Fifth, lightly pat and rub the inner and outer thighs and calves. Sixth, form loose fists and pat the buttocks. Seventh, make circles with your knees by placing your hands on the kneecaps. Eighth, rotate the ankles, one foot at a time. Lastly, squat down and stand up a few times. Finish up by marching in place until the breath becomes even again.

"This is a version of the preparatory exercises for meditation that has been modified and simplified for modern times. In the

---

49 六字訣 (*liuzijue*). The term was first mentioned by Tao Hongjing (420–589 CE) in his book *On Caring for the Health of the Mind and Prolonging the Life Span*. He was a Daoist master and an alchemist, and was very knowledgeable in Traditional Chinese Medicine.

past, Daoist priests who lived in the mountains all used a similar set of exercises before meditation. There are two other sets that can also be practiced before beginning a session, namely the 8- and 12-section brocades. These are very effective methods for regulating and balancing the body."

CHAPTER **16**

TOTAL RELAXATION: WITHOUT ATTACHMENT TO ANY PLACE

Sifu said: "At the time when I was still fresh in my meditation training, there was another young man at the Daoist temple who had recently been initiated as a priest. He couldn't have been more than 20 years of age and was also, like myself, training in meditation. One day while talking to us, our master said we should practice together."

Without pausing for a breath, *sifu* moved from the meditation warmup exercises he had just been teaching and started talking about the period when he had been studying the Dao on Qingcheng Mountain.

"During that time, I would doggedly follow the young priest and sit whenever he meditated. Sometimes we would sit through the whole morning! Blame it on our youthful energy," he smiled.

"At that time I would experience various physical sensations. When I first started, my bowels would move with gusto, and loud sounds would slowly rumble up from my stomach. At times I would feel the sensation of energy traveling all the way up to the space between my eyebrows. My vision would frequently fill with light—regardless of whether my eyes were closed or open— followed by a buzzing, a droning in my ears that would fade and reappear suddenly like a busy bee. Later this would develop into an incessant buzz within my ears that would continue for the whole day. I found this greatly unsettling and perplexing.

"I asked my daily practice partner, the young priest, about the things that were happening to me. When he replied that he had experienced nothing of the sort, we sought out the advice of our master. The strange sensations I described seemed not to shock our master in the least. He told me, coolly: 'When meditating, relax your mind and body as much as possible. Do not let your mind fixate on any part of the body, especially any of the acupoints. Before you receive instructions on these points, do not let your mind linger on any one spot. Seeing lights and ringing in your ears is all related to having placed your attention entirely on your head. All you need to do next time is divert your attention to the lower abdomen or the soles of your feet and you'll be fine. Your body definitely should not feel taut when meditating. You must be mentally and physically relaxed. With regards to your mental state, maintain an attitude of letting things happen naturally. When distracting thoughts come, let them come. When they stop, let them stop. The host follows the whims of the guests without paying heed to anything, and pays them no attention once they've left. This is the first step in relaxation."

Sifu continued: "The most vital life essence within our physical bodies is gathered in the area around the navel, especially in the *qihai*. The *qihai* encompasses the entire area under the navel and is one of the locations on which we should place our focus during meditation. It is the core, the control center of our body. You could compare it to the deep foundations of a skyscraper, or the frame of a towering pagoda. This is exactly why we learn to focus on the *dantian* during meditation. An even more important point above the navel is the *huangting*. If there is a qualified person willing to reveal the location of this point, and we combine this knowledge with mind training, the keys to unlocking humanity's greatest source of innate potential will come within our grasp."

CHAPTER 17

LIFE HINGES ON THE BREATH

Sifu said: "The average person is unable to control and maintain the balance of their physical condition. They must depend on the intake of water, vegetation, sunlight, and various foods to nourish and sustain the body. If the innate potential that lies within them has not been uncovered, they would have no way to explore the extraordinary power of techniques involving the breath. Those who have trained in the *qi* exercises connected with inhalation and exhalation, on the other hand, are able to expel impure *qi* and carbon dioxide from their bodies. They achieve this through the transformation of blood that enters the arteries from the veins and capillaries, simply by inhaling pure oxygen.

"According to medical studies, under normal conditions a person takes over 20,000 breaths daily. If you practiced meditation and absorbed the fresh air inhaled through these techniques, it would have a significant purifying effect on your blood. A whole array of illnesses are rooted in the blood, and blood and breath are directly connected. If you are inhaling correctly, the oxygen absorbed into your body is rich and nourishing and will aid in the circulation of your blood, which is, after all, directly involved in the healthy operation of your stomach, intestines, and the five viscera.

"The reason I keep bringing up the breath and the *dantian* is because all of the body's responses are directly related to these two elements. Knowledge of the breath is such a broad field. With it, you could bring your breath under control and in so doing control all of nature.

"My Daoist master, for example, would sit in meditative stillness for three months at a time when he was practicing in the Yandang Mountains.[50] The entrance of his retreat cave would be blocked

---

50   雁荡山. A coastal mountain range in southeastern Zhejiang province in eastern China.

off by a makeshift, wooden door sealed shut with a giant lock on the outside. A tiny sliver of space was left under the door for his attendant from the Daoist temple to place his meals. Only after 100 days would the retreat warden unlock the door, signaling the end of his retreat.

"The funny thing is, every day when the attendant delivered the food, the meal from the previous day would be sitting on the ground, untouched. The line of bowls would just grow longer and longer until the end of the week, when the attendant would have no choice but to take them away.

"Once my master entered into a state of meditative stillness, he would remain within this state and wouldn't eat. He told me that his Daoist lineage had passed down oral tips on meditation and that many before him had had profound experiences after putting them into practice. My master's own master, for example, only consumed liquids and never ate solid foods. Despite this, he was always full of energy, with more strength than an able man half his age, a voice that resounded like a bell, and eyes that shone like coins. He would walk as if flying, and always looked fresh and in high spirits. At that time my master said to me: 'Life hinges on the breath.' Through daily practice, my understanding of these words has grown.

"The breath is critical. When the next one never comes, a person's time on this earth ends. I always make a point to spend as much time as necessary explaining the breath to anyone new to Daoist meditation. We all know two types of breathing: exhalation and inhalation. But it gets more interesting if you examine one of the Chinese characters for breath. The top portion of the character, *zi*, means 'oneself' and the bottom portion, *xin*, means 'mind.' This shows the unmistakable connection between the breath and the mind.

"The saying 'The mind and breath are interdependent' actually hints at the secret to the highest state of meditation. In this state, there is neither inhalation nor exhalation—all that remains is the highest, singular, original mind. The breath becomes a single thread of *qi*, a *qi* that takes on a much greater purpose!"

CHAPTER 18

YOU ARE THE MASTER OF YOUR LIFE

Sifu and I had talked for so long that I hadn't even noticed the time. It was already past noon. Usually people took turns providing meals for *sifu* and the students that visited on holidays. One of the people in charge of the kitchen was Xiaoqing, a woman and student of *sifu's* who had once worked in the restaurant business. She later became very ill and was taken to see *sifu* by some of his students. Through acupuncture and herbal medicine, *sifu* slowly restored her to health. During her recovery process, *sifu* had insisted on her meditating every day for 15–30 minutes as well as practicing the posting stance that he had taught her. Through these, she was able to defeat her seemingly incurable disease.

In her old age and out of gratitude toward *sifu*, she had decided to dedicate her time to volunteering in the temple's kitchen. I once heard her say that *sifu* himself ate next-to-nothing, only a tiny portion of daily vegetables. Even more incredible is that he would never actually swallow his food; he would just chew the vegetables in his mouth and spit them out into a bowl. There was a period of time during which *sifu* had altogether abandoned chewable food, drinking only certain foods specially ground into a juice. On top of that, he would spend 100 days every year practicing the secret oral tips of the *Yellow Court Classic* in his retreat cave in the Yuli Mountains.[51]

Every time *sifu* went on his mountain retreat he would survive on nothing but water for 100 days. Despite his diet, he never seemed worse for wear. When once asked by a concerned student as to whether this retreat diet would end up adversely affecting

---

51 玉里山. A mountainous area in northern Taiwan.

his health, he simply responded: "There's no need to worry about these things. A true Daoist practitioner needs only to practice and observe Daoist breathing and fasting techniques to connect oneself with the universe, thus prolonging his lifespan. You have all heard of the story of Zuo Ci (169–280 CE) and what he did after obtaining the oral instructions in *Nine Pills Golden Saliva*.[52] He secluded himself in retreat on Mount Tianzhu,[53] practicing silent contemplation as a means of communicating with the Daoist deities. Once he acquired supernatural abilities, he was able to summon all manner of spirits. Word of him reached Cao Cao,[54] the dynasty's commanding warlord. Cao Cao requested Zuo Ci's appearance at court with an offering of an official title and beautiful women, both of which Zuo Ci refused. In his fury, Cao Cao locked Zuo Ci in a stone cell and stationed guards outside. Zuo Ci was held for an entire year without food and only one daily cup of water for sustenance.

"After one year Cao Cao suddenly remembered this character whom they had kept locked up, and sent someone to bring him to the royal court. The moment Cao Cao laid eyes on Zuo Ci, he was shocked. He thought to himself that this person had not eaten anything for a whole year, yet somehow here he was, inconceivably glowing with radiance. Could it be possible, Cao Cao thought, that the rumors were true, that standing before him was a living Daoist immortal? This spurred even more desire in Cao Cao to bring him under his command, but Zuo Ci politely and repeatedly refused. Cao Cao, having taken another blow to his ego, thought to do away with him. Feigning politeness, Cao Cao poisoned a cup of wine and offered Zuo Ci a farewell drink. Zuo Ci, knowing the ruse, produced a hidden dagger from under his robe and by stirring the drink, the dagger promptly broke in two. Cao Cao flew into a rage and told the soldiers to grab a sword, but the Daoist had vanished into the crowd."

---

52 九丹金液 (*Jiudanjinye*). A Daoist classic.
53 天柱山. Anhui, China.
54 曹操 (c. 155–220 CE). Chinese warlord and Chancellor of the Eastern Han dynasty. A central figure of the Three Kingdoms period, posthumously honored as "Emperor Wu of Wei." Subsequent literature praised him as a brilliant ruler and military genius who treated his subordinates like family.

CHAPTER 19

TIPS FOR A LONG, HEALTHY LIFE

Sifu continued: "We receive a considerable amount of life essence while in our mother's womb via the umbilical cord. A great deal of this precious life energy is used up after birth by the emotions and afflictions swirling around in our mind. However, if we knew how to return to our true selves and regain the natural state, and how to practice the Dao and train in stillness, we could gradually unearth and release the primordial energy hidden within every one of us. This, in turn, would strengthen our vitality.

"In my hometown there lives a man known as 'Old Man Chen' who is over 150 years old. He isn't a monk. He claims only that when he was young he received instructions regarding the 12 *qi* bathing exercises[55] for extending life and the *shouqiao* technique of meditation from a highly achieved Daoist abbot. He just practiced what the abbot had taught him every day. To his own surprise, he crept over 100 years of age still full of energy. His beard and eyebrows may have turned white, but the wrinkles on his face were not as deep as they are for most old people. Furthermore, when he spoke he was witty, and he had an infectious sense of humor that would leave people with a very positive feeling.

"When asked what his secret to a long life was, he answered: 'I don't usually drink, never smoke, don't get angry, forget whatever I hear, only think of the good in others, don't hold grudges or have bad intentions toward others and don't compete. If someone wants my seat, I give it to them. I don't start bickering if they get mad at me. All my thoughts are about joyful and happy things. I don't mull over whatever happened during the day as I'm about to sleep; I just happily drift off to sleep.'"

---

55 十二長生沐浴功法 (*shierchangshengmuyugongfa*). A *qigong* practice for purifying the body.

Then *sifu* paused to reflect and said: "There was also an old Daoist abbot called Li Qingyun who lived to be over 200 years old. The reason these people were able to prolong their lives was their ability to manage their minds and breath a little better than the normal person. The reason most people get sick, and why a young person might pass on at an early age, is also due to wasting too much energy without being able to restore it."

CHAPTER 20

A RARE GLIMPSE OF
EXTRAORDINARY DAOIST FEATS

As I recall, *sifu* never spoke much. Aside from the lessons which required his personal instruction, he kept his words brief. The basic techniques of Daoist practice—including meditation, posting stances, taiji,[56] staff, *Xingyi,*[57] *Bagua,*[58] internal martial arts, and *daoyin*[59]—were overseen by his more senior students. Throughout his life, he never attended a single funeral or wedding, and he never visited women if they had recently given birth. He kept silent and taciturn apart from when he would receive the occasional visit from fellow practitioners passing through Taiwan. They would dabble in a game of chess, discuss poetry, or exchange their views and experiences on the path of Daoist practice. I expect that his inner stillness remained constant at all times.

But there was the occasion, when the mood took him, that words would flow like a fountain. Sometimes he would talk for an entire afternoon.

One particular situation seemed to have piqued *sifu*'s interest. He related: "It was during a year I spent in Chengdu[60] that I met a Daoist practitioner. The man kept to himself. He was an unkempt fellow and ate everything, regardless of whether it was vegetarian or otherwise. He would often sound deranged when he talked. But he was someone who truly knew the Dao, as I would find out that winter.

---

56 太極拳 (taiji). An internal Chinese martial art practiced for health benefits and as an applied fighting style.

57 形意. A martial arts system, which translates approximately as "Form-Intention Fist," or "Shape-Will Fist."

58 八卦. A martial arts system organized around the eight trigrams.

59 導引. A series of exercises practiced by Daoists to cultivate internal energy.

60 成都. The capital of southwest China's Sichuan province.

"How did I find out? On cold winter evenings everyone in the city would go out covered from head to toe in full cotton-lined coats, scarves, and caps. This gentleman, however, would walk around in a thin overcoat, seemingly unaffected by the chill.

"I once saw him treat someone with a serious illness. The only tool he used was his three fingers, with which he traced the major acupoints on the patient's body. To cries of 'It's really hot!' I saw steam rise from the places where he touched. I have actually met many such practitioners who could do this.

"I was in the habit of looking into every nook and cranny for Daoist practitioners of great ability. If I heard of one, regardless of how far away they might be, regardless of whether the stories about them were true or not, or whether the person truly walked the path of the Dao, I would always find them and present them with offerings.

"There was one Daoist practitioner named Gong from the Northeast. Of his own account, when he was still young he met with a Daoist practitioner in North *Wutai*[61] and stayed with him for seven years. From this master swordsman Mr. Gong learned the skill of '*qi* driving the sword.'[62]

"Once he attained mastery, I asked him one day for a demonstration.

"He led me outside. It was the second or third day of the lunar year. There were light flurries in the air, a rare sight in Sichuan province. That year, I remember that it had snowed without pause from the beginning of the lunar new year. As we walked through the snow, to my surprise I noticed that Mr. Gong had not left a single footprint. In all likelihood he wasn't even aware that he had let this little secret slip.

"Outside there was a row of osmanthus and gingko trees draped in snow, like they had been decorated for Christmas. Mr. Gong walked with his eyes closed, focusing on the trunks of a few trees, slightly taller than a man. He took a deep breath and promptly expelled the air from his nose. Upon his third forceful exhalation, all the snow on the tree ten paces ahead instantly melted.

61　北五台. Sacred Buddhist site in Shanxi province, China.
62　氣馭劍 (*qiyujian*). The practice of using the intention as a sword.

"I was dumbstruck. I told myself that I would drop to my hands and knees the next chance I got and ask to be taken on as a student. I returned with Mr. Gong to his room with just such an intention, but just as I started to bend in obeisance, Mr. Gong's toes were already pressing against my kneecap. 'There is no need for that,' he said. 'I have never taken a disciple. It will be enough for us to be fellow practitioners.' He had outmaneuvered me.

"This was just one of the extraordinary people I met that year. Looking back, it seems a shame that I didn't ask to be taken as a disciple a few more times. Who knows how many years it has been? So many things have changed, and this practitioner seems to have wandered into the fog of history. My thirst for this form of martial art only grew with time, but despite having been introduced by fellow practitioners to some of the most capable masters alive, I was unable to fulfill my desires."

SINGLE-POINTED FOCUS TO EMPTY ALL DISTRACTED THOUGHTS

Sifu continued: "Fortunately, after my missed opportunity I still managed to run into one of the outstanding disciples of Liu Zhitan. This student was a famous Chinese Medicine doctor surnamed Qian, then known as 'the fire god master.' I would meet with him regularly, and he would later become one of my close friends.

"Doctor Qian told me about how his teacher, Liu Zhitan, had first come across the respected Master Yeyun, a meeting that led to almost ten years of study. During this time he experienced immense progress in his health, scholarship, and wisdom, in particular excelling in practicing the oral tips of internal alchemy.

"The doctor assured me that he had never met anyone like Master Liu before. At that time he was already a legend. He was adept in the three schools of Confucianism, Daoism, and Buddhism, and had written a stack of books taller than himself. His influence in the scholarly world was widespread.

"Master Liu's *sifu* came into his life at just the right time. He had become severely ill after failing the imperial examination. What's more, his *sifu* came in the most unassuming form of an old man selling herbal plasters and was known as 'Master Yeyun.' When Master Liu set his eyes upon this old man, he saw something extraordinary. He saw a man far along the path of the Dao. Upon requesting a way to extend his life, the old man, hurriedly, rattled off a few words: 'Maintain a virtuous mind to cultivate your moral nature,'[63] a presumably simple oral tip for the combined practice

---

63 存心養氣，存心養性 (*cunxinyangqi, cunxinyangxing*). Literally, maintain spirit by cultivating *qi*, maintain spirit by cultivating essence.

of body and mind.[64] After years residing with the elderly man and exerting himself to the utmost, Master Liu obtained the essence of Daoist internal alchemy. All of his chronic ailments were swept away, and from the age of 60 to 80, he fathered eight sons—truly a testament to the value of meditation and the practice of internal alchemy."[65]

The rain outside began to fall heavily. *Sifu* and I moved to the office where he usually received guests. I made a cup of his customary *longjing* tea, and having taken a sip, the respected elder resumed his narrative:

"Doctor Qian himself was quite blessed to meet the great master Liu Zhitan, known in those days as 'the old scholar.' After we had become good friends, we would often mutually share what we had learned about the practice of stillness and Daoism. He told me that the greatest oral tip for the practice of meditation and the discipline of 'golden *dantian*' of Liu's school consisted of these few words: 'singular focus on the internal meditation points.' Gradually, one may enter into the state of 'Nothingness,' within which you experience a state of unborn awareness,[66] and this is the core of the practice."

Master told me that during his time at the Daoist Temple, his master had once told him: "When you practice to a certain point,[67] you will be able to enjoy a long life, longevity. This is the technique you should apply to your current stage of practice. If, while following your breath during meditation, you find yourself barely able to detect your in-breath, this indicates the gradual fading of distracted, delusive thoughts. This is exactly the time to apply the method of focusing on a single point. In modern terms, this singular focus is the unity of your essence and spirit. You don't

---

64 性命雙修 (*xingmingshuangxiu*). Sometimes translated as "combined practice of spirit and body" or "essence and nature"; that is, to cultivate essence through practices that involve one's disposition and overall vitality, or to cultivate nature through practices that involve one's body and *qi*. Both are internal alchemy practices in Daoism.

65 煉丹 (*liandan*). Referring to the internal practices.

66 一炁 (*yiqi*). Refers to the primordial state of not arising, not ceasing.

67 服丹守一, 壽與天齊, 回金入息, 壽至無極 (*fudanshouyi, shouyutianqi, huijinruqi, shouzhiwuji*). Daoist longevity practice that involves ingesting certain materials, refining mental states, and returning to fetal breathing.

have to do anything more than lightly place your attention on a single object or on the breath. Never use a heavy-handed, forced approach."

Sifu looked as if he had just remembered something, and said: "Just now I was speaking of Master Liu's particular school of techniques. I had initially asked Dr. Qian whether there was any difference between Liu's school and the other Daoist branches. Doctor Qian told me: 'When Master Liu was teaching, I never felt anything special in his instructions. It was all very simple.'"

Sifu continued to elaborate on Dr. Qian's description of the practice: "'Sit in a relaxed, posture with the legs crossed. Then, clench the fists and place them on either side of the navel with the palms facing up. Keep the mouth closed and lightly press the tongue to where the upper palate meets the the teeth. Through suggestion, empty all distracting thoughts from your mind. Direct your eyes and your intention to the middle of the chest and follow up by lightly clacking the teeth together 36 times. When this is done, once again empty your mind. Swash around the saliva in your mouth until it is full, then swallow it down to the *dantian*. After that, again inspect whether or not your mind has any stray thoughts. Lightly place your awareness on the *dantian*. Let your mind become as broad and vast as space, while keeping it from drifting or wavering. If a thought arises, lightly swallow a bit of saliva. If thoughts constantly emerge as you sit in meditation, simply pay them no due. It's important not to make yourself uncomfortable by tensing up or over-exerting yourself.'"

Sifu continued: "In due time I came to realize that the essence of Master Liu's school of teaching resides in reflective insight[68] and its two methods for penetrating focus.[69] One of the methods is to direct your gaze toward the *dantian* while lightly swallowing a mouthful of saliva and sending it to that region. The other one is the same, but with eyes closed while still directed at this spot. If distracting thoughts arise during your meditation, softly bringing your attention back to the *dantian* will suffice."

---

68 觀照 (*guanzhao*). Enlightenment as the result of insight or intelligent contemplation.
69 專照 (*zhuanzhao*).

Despite the widespread popularity of Master Liu and his school of teaching, *sifu* said he was later able to summarize Liu's methods into one pithy phrase: "Concentrate the mind on a single place." In other words, there is no point in cutting off various, distracted thoughts. Whether you are walking, still, or sleeping, always bring your attention to the *dantian* whenever distracted thoughts arise. If you have no distracted thoughts or delusive thinking, then so much the better—cultivate your internal alchemy. Lightly hold your focus on the *dantian*.

Sifu then told me: "Although this meditation method can give rise to wondrous effects, one cannot become too attached to it. Besides, I believe that, despite all of Dr. Liu's study, he hasn't really seen the whole picture. This is because in all the years that I was around him, I cannot say I saw any areas in which he distinguished himself from others, although it can indeed be said that his bodily condition and his complexion showed that he had practiced austerities to a much higher level than the common man. It's a pity that he later got busy involved in running his clinic—periods of diligent practice were sparse from that point on. This is actually a juncture that practitioners will often come across."

CHAPTER 22

START EARLY AND NEVER
ABANDON THE WILL
TO WALK THE PATH

Sifu at once became solemn. He said: "The sooner you engage in the study and practice of Daoism, the better. Do not waste time on worthless activities. The years are as fleeting as the spark from a flint or a flash of lightning. You must cherish every second, and squeeze every drop out of your short time here. Have no desire for all the fame and riches of the world.

"There is one point especially: On the path of the Dao, you will encounter many obstacles and hardships. But you must never lose your will to find the Dao. You must not give up halfway. Remain eager and diligent in learning even into old age. Understand that in order to obtain the supreme method for producing 'The way of the golden pill,'[70] to return to the roots of your being,[71] restore the essence of your life, and achieve a state replete with spirit and energy, you must strive until your last breath.

"Look at our forefather Ge Hong, who only started on the path at the age of 60, or Master Lu Dongbin, who only met his master at 54. There's also Zhang Sanfeng, who persevered in his austerities until he was 70 years old, finally obtaining the highest state of immortality.[72]

---

70 金丹之道 (*jindanzhidao*). The path of the golden pill was originally a technique used for making an external pill of longevity. Later, after the Tang and Song dynasties, it was brought into use as a technique for the internal pill of longevity. Thus, it refers to the Daoist practice method for the cultivation of the inner, or "golden" pill.

71 歸根復命 (*guigenfuming*). Return to the roots, the beginning of life by learning to breathe through the *dantian*.

72 大羅天仙 (*daluotianxian*). The highest level of Daoist alchemical achievement. "Immortality" in the Daoist sense does not imply eternal life but rather an extended life span, numbered in the hundreds.

"My master knew a fellow practitioner who was once a high-ranking military official. At 75, the fragility of his years suddenly dawned upon him. He took leave of his wife and children and went to the mountain to beg Master Tai to accept him as a student. Master Tai obliged, and transmitted the methods of immortality to him.

"From the moment he left home to enter the Dao, not once did he rest. From morning to night he remained fixed in meditation. Before the year was through, he had made phenomenal progress. Master Tai was pleasantly surprised, for he knew that this relationship had been predestined from a past life. It was with this in mind that Master Tai imparted the key oral instructions of his school to the former military man. Who could have imagined that in the span of a single three-year retreat, he would go so far as to open completely his governing and conception channels? We can see here that the path of spiritual practice bears only the resolute. You would do well to remember everything I have said, lest old age come bearing only regret."

CHAPTER 23

WHAT SURPRISES MODERN MEDICINE UNEARTHED

Sifu continued his heartfelt words, saying: "From their first to their last breath, humans will inevitably go through the process of disease and death. In the future, when you pass the threshold of your 40s, you will come to feel it clearly for yourself. Your immune system and various organs will start going noticeably downhill. Focus on making good use of your heart and kidneys. If you can maintain healthy kidney function, your organs should be fine into your 80s and even 90s. The heart is the fulcrum which governs the body's entire blood system. If you practice meditation to cultivate the pill of immortality so as to keep the heart and kidneys in top condition, achieving longevity and immortality is not out of reach.

"From a medical perspective, meditation aids both the metabolism and the endocrine system—the system that regulates our body's secretion of hormones.

"Two major players in the aging process are hormones and the pituitary gland. Weighing in at less than a gram at the base of the skull, the pituitary gland's central role is the secretion of hormones—and therefore its profound effect on us is often overlooked. The activation of this gland, along with the hypothalamus, leads to the release of many types of hormones. The secretion of growth hormones, for example, has an effect on the metabolism of our daily intake of carbohydrates and proteins, in turn affecting our bones and muscles. There are serious consequences when this hormonal system—known as the endocrine system—becomes imbalanced. An excess or deficiency of normal hormone levels can change our physical appearance. It can also affect our psychology and physiology on a number of levels.

"Another problem I often see is people who suffer from overactive or sluggish thyroid glands. This has a great impact on the body and mind, especially for middle-aged women. It may even alter their personality. These issues are all related to the hormones produced by the pituitary gland and in serious cases can even affect the health of the womb, ovaries, and breasts.

"The simple solution to all of these problems is meditation.

"Medical organizations all over the world are discovering that the cerebellum, the endocrine system, and the metabolism are primarily responsible for our health. Experiments on animals have led to these and other great discoveries.

"After World War II, many Westerners began to take an interest in Eastern mysticism. When I was practicing in the mountains, I came across four of them myself. They were German and French. They had gone to China specifically to learn of the mysteries of Daoism. Two of them even went on to become Daoist priests and experts on China.

"After applying themselves to the physical practices, they were surprised to discover that, without the aid of medicine, their chronic illnesses had vanished. This only served to solidify their faith in meditation and Daoist longevity pills. After this, many scientific and medical groups from the West made the trip to Mount Qingcheng to visit and study.

"Once, I happened to catch a small team of researchers who had come seeking an understanding of *qigong*. The team, hailing from three different countries, asked two of the Daoist temple priests to demonstrate some of their skills while they took measurements. First, they taped a feather under the nostrils of one priest. He took a breath and held it in his *dantian* for the entire afternoon. The feather never so much as stirred. They hooked the other priest up to a blood pressure meter, a heart rate monitor, and some other advanced medical equipment. From the readings, they were able to watch as he brought his heart to a complete stop. He could also control his pulse at will. Needless to say, it was quite a shock to the visitors from the West!"

My *sifu* spoke kindly and with great consideration: "I have been instructing you through the stages of meditation and the microcosmic orbit, exactly as my *sifu* imparted these same practices to me. When I was studying, I consistently worked into the night and was taxed mentally and physically. My schedule and routine was completely backward, which was all the more reason for me to make time to visit the Daoist temple. I needed the visits to settle my mind and ask the priest how to be rid of everything vexing me. Perhaps owing to poor diet, I contracted tuberculosis. Tuberculosis could be considered the 'Black Plague' of our century."

CHAPTER 24

THE TONGUE'S UNCANNY ROLE IN COLLECTING THE MIND

Sifu continued: "When it comes to meditation, people tend to emphasize the importance of sitting cross-legged and other physical postures. One of the more commonly known methods— the 'Seven-Point Meditation' method—involves seven particulars on how to sit properly. It is, however, simply a foundation. There were so many differing views on its finer points amongst the practitioners on the mountain that we never dwelled long on it. Don't misunderstand me: Beginners should learn all of the ins and outs of how to cross the legs, how to adjust the spine, shoulders and head, and where to fix the gaze. Physical cues become less relevant for those who move on to cultivate *qi* and enter a state of stillness. At this point, all you need to do is keep your legs in a position that is stable and comfortable for you.

"Beginners to meditation should always prop themselves up 3–5 centimeters off the ground with a soft cushion. The cushion should neither be too soft nor made of impermeable, artificial material such as man-made sponge. This will block the natural flow of *qi*, resulting in poor circulation. A cushion made of coconut husk covered by cotton fabric provides the right amount of cushioning and permeability without irritating the skin. Sitting with your bottom slightly elevated allows you to stay in the posture for longer periods of time.

"Elongate your spine without too much exertion. Too much strain will cause your fire *qi* to rise.[73] Gentle reminders to naturally

---

73 火氣上升 (*huoqishangsheng*). In Chinese Medicine, fire is one of the pernicious influences that cause the body to become imbalanced or ill. When excessive, it can easily rise in the body and cause disruption and illness. Typical reactions are insomnia, excessive dreams, feeling of heat, irritability, etc.

keep the spine straight are enough to do the trick. Relax your shoulders so they naturally give in to gravity. Tilt your head slightly forward, about 15 degrees, and gently tuck in your chin. This will apply pressure to the two major arteries in the neck. The afflictions and delusive thoughts spinning around in your head are directly connected to these two arteries. Softly applying pressure to them by tucking in the chin calms the mind and spirit.

"Keep the eyes relaxed, about halfway between open and closed. The Daoist term for this is 'draping the curtain.' This is another way of describing the position the eyelids naturally assume when we let them drop—but not so much that we shut out our spirit. The eyes are, after all, the gateways to the mind and spirit, and when they are fully closed, delusive thoughts subsequently arise. The only time it is advisable to fully close the eyes is if our mind is overactive and we need to take a minute to regulate the breath and restore our spirit.

"The best way to maintain an open mind while meditating is by keeping the eyes half open, collecting your thoughts and lightly pressing the tip of your tongue against the roof of the mouth, behind the top teeth. The longer you sit, the further your tongue will naturally curl back, generating saliva. Do not underestimate the wondrous effect the tongue's position here can bring about! It can result in what is known in Daoism as 'connecting the magpie bridge,' the meaning of which you will grasp as your experience deepens. Once the connection to the 'magpie bridge' is unblocked, according to Daoism, the conception and governing channels will open. As to the purpose of wiggling the base of the tongue to further stimulate the secretion of saliva, I will explain this later, when we get to the stage of cultivating the *dantian*."

A younger meditator's constitution and abundance of original essence makes it easy to quickly generate saliva through this exercise. Once the tongue becomes limber and the mouth is filled, some people may experience a warm, vibrating sensation in their *dantian*. Young meditators may then feel this surge of warm *qi* flowing continuously around the lower belly and kidneys. This is purely beginner's luck.

Those who are older will require an extended period of meditation before they feel a warming sensation in their *dantian*.

For those who tend to produce less saliva, curling the tip of the tongue as previously mentioned will help. You may use the same methods when you feel bothered and irritated, or if you find yourself in an extremely dry climate. Placing the tip of the tongue on your palate, you will soon be able to feel calm again, and even less thirsty. Slowly swallow the saliva produced, and you will regain your physical and mental balance.

The condition of the tongue and its coating tell a Traditional Chinese Medicine (TCM) doctor a lot about a patient's health. By examining the color, coating, and teeth marks left on its surface, most TCM doctors will be able to identify problems in the corresponding internal organs. I usually combine breathing techniques with the aforementioned movement involving the tip of tongue touching the roof of the mouth, then rolling it back and tucking in the chin. Doing so helps alleviate fatigue, and always leaves me feeling refreshed and invigorated. I have shared and taught this meditation technique to many people experiencing issues with their intestinal tract and stomach. After using it for an extended period of time, most of them found that gastrointestinal problems miraculously vanished. In truth, it is the work of the enzymes in saliva produced during meditation.

CHAPTER 25

HEALTH IS ON THE TIP OF YOUR FINGERS

Let the hands rest on the thighs near the area of the lower *dantian*. Bring the tips of the thumbs lightly together to help keep the mind focused on a single point.

Our ten fingers, especially the thumbs, have their counterparts in the mind. The tips of the fingers are also connected to the five organs and six viscera. Starting with the thumbs, we can trace a circuit to the brain, which is why touching them together at the tip helps quieten our thoughts. Massaging them regularly also helps. The index finger is correlated with the digestive system (stomach and intestine), the middle finger with the heart, the ring finger with the liver, and the pinky finger with the kidneys. During sitting meditation, you can massage all of your fingers to support the healthy function of your five organs.

A few days ago, a woman was in the middle of sitting meditation when she felt the onset of a pounding headache. All of the blood and *qi* had rushed to her head. I instructed one of the other meditators to administer acupuncture on her thumbs and other pertinent points. Soon after, her blood pressure came back down. This is just one example of how basic principles of good health can be effective, even when acute symptoms arise.

If you have a weak digestive system, as well as bloating and episodes of diarrhea, then regularly massaging the index fingers will help. If the area around your heart and chest often feels stuffy, constricted or painful, massage your thumbs and middle fingers. If you have poor cardiopulmonary function, or have trouble breathing, massage the ring fingers. If you have weak kidneys, your lower back gets sore, or you have poor *qi* and blood circulation, massage the pinky fingers.

On a side note, the color of our nails is also a clear indicator of our health and, upon closer observation, gives us a way to know our body better. Some people, for example, might see a dark purplish color suddenly appear under the nail. This is likely an early warning sign of impending complications with blood vessels in the brain, which could lead to a stroke. If there is black discoloration, seek medical attention as soon as possible, especially if the color persists. This is not something you should just ignore: Research, statistics, and past medical records have shown that malignant diseases manifest themselves on the nails in the form of black discoloration or patches.

CHAPTER 26

MIND AND *QI* ARE FREED IN COMPLETE RELAXATION

Besides the postures for sitting as explained above, relaxing from head to toe is as important here as it might be in taiji. When I first learned the movements of taiji from an instructor directed by my Daoist master, it was only after practicing for months that its subtle power was revealed.

The instructor first told me to "lift my arms naturally." I puzzled a great while over what kind of lifting I would have to do to be "natural." Then it occurred to me that when the body is floating on the ocean, it has the ability to be in a state of total relaxation. The more relaxed the body is, the less restricted. I visualized the "emptiness" of my body from the crown of my head all the way to the toes. To my amazement, when I breathed into my *dantian*, my hands floated up of their own accord.

When I got to the final stages of my martial arts training, my movements were completely the result of energy vibrations. Everything was done with intention, but without force. Where there is intention, there is *qi*. When intention and *qi* are connected, the force of the movement arises.

I had a Daoist friend living in Shanghai. He was at a dinner party and everyone was clamoring to see his ability to make things levitate. He had no choice but to give them what they wanted. To just witness him taking a breath was amazing—the utensils on the table soared into the air, and the tablecloth draped over the Eight-Immortals table[74] was whipped off before all the bowls and plates quietly settled back to their places. This was an incredible

---

74　八仙桌 (*baxianzhuo*). The table had carvings of the Eight Immortals, considered to be signs of prosperity and longevity.

display from a highly accomplished taiji master, which I witnessed first-hand.

Sifu once told me that in taiji the only things left are flowery displays of fists and fancy footwork, with nothing that could be considered "martial arts." This is owing to the work of taiji master Yang Luchan (19th century). He kept some of the teachings hidden and designed a superficial set to give to the old ladies and maids of the palace. In order to practice real taiji, you must have a foundation of internal martial arts. You must have *qi* before you can bring out the true power of the practice. You must be able to walk as if the ground were made of cotton, and sit as if you were dangling from strings like a puppet.

Daoist practitioners pay particular attention to the *qi* and to intention; they do not emphasize movements or the postures of the body. If too much attention is put on the body and its movements, it can lead to *qi* stagnation. Once the *qi* stagnates, the practice will stagnate. There are many modern meditation postures that can scramble and unravel your *qi*, or even lead to illness if you are not careful. Furthermore, we shouldn't relax to the point of the chest becoming stuffy or the back rounding. If this happens, the *qi* in the back will stagnate. This can lead to bone spurs, or the *qi* may stagnate so severely that it is no longer able to disperse or flow out. If too much force is used to level the shoulders, the *qi* and blood will rush upward to the head. The *qi* may also become stagnant in the back of the head, causing heaviness in the head, headaches, trigeminal neuralgia, migraines, or similar problems.

CHAPTER **27**

MEDITATION IS NOT AN EXERCISE FOR THE LEGS

Many people ask about lengthening the period of time they are able to sit in the lotus posture. Such concerns shouldn't be given too much time. We all have a limited number of years to spend in this world. Don't spend it on questions like this. I've seen people squander a lifetime working on the condition of their legs. By the time the *qi* and blood are unobstructed and the capacity to maintain full lotus for a period of time is available, it is nearly time to move on to the next world. This is not a good use of time. We can't compete with trees, rocks, tables, or chairs. What do they get from 100 or even 1,000 years of sitting still? This way, there will be no chance to attain enlightenment, to develop wisdom, or to practice the combined cultivation of body and mind.

For those more advanced in years, I advise sitting on a wooden bench. It will be enough if the feet can make contact with the *qi* of the earth. Another method is to sit on raised cushions, high enough to avoid pain, numbness, or other discomfort in the legs.

After sitting in meditation for a short while, some people will feel the *qi* has begun to move. They may interpret this as a sign of the conception and governing channels opening. Those who understand the *qigong* practice of dynamic tension won't give such physical experiences a second thought. For those with a sensitive constitution, anxiety or stiff muscles, after some breathing practices, they will relax and loosen up considerably. Naturally, the *qi* will start to move, but this has nothing to do with the micro- and macrocosmic orbits.[75]

75　小周天, 大周天 (*xiaozhoutian, dazhoutian*). Daoist practices that involve moving the *qi* through channels in an "orbit" around the body.

In the beginning, when setting a foundation for meditation practice, sit in a natural, cross-legged position, relax the entire body, and keep the eyes half open. Set the eyes on any point 3–5 meters ahead without straining. Over-exertion may cause the eyes to feel swollen. This may even create the false impression that the eyes have developed a sort of supernatural power. Most importantly, keep the mind relaxed; if it wanders, bring it back. At first, there is no need to put focus on any specific point. Whatever experiences come, disregard them.

The abundance of *yang qi*[76] in younger people makes it easier to kindle and rise during meditation. In the case of men, this can manifest as an erection. At this time, relax the entire body, tightly clench the teeth, place the tongue on the upper palate and direct the eyes toward the genitals. Do not give rise to any feelings of desire, and slowly the erection will subside. The *dantian* will have a feeling of warmth. And after continued meditation, the essence, *qi* and spirit will gradually be transformed into original essence, original *qi* and original spirit.

---

76   陽氣. Masculine aspect, from the balanced dichotomy of *yin* and *yang*.

CHAPTER **28**

THE COSMOS FOLDED INTO ONE

Impatience is an enemy to meditation practice. In the past, there was a young Daoist priest who came up the mountain to seek the Dao.[77] My teacher saw that he was healthy and spirited, but feared that he lacked perseverance. For several days, this Daoist priest kneeled before the temple gate. My teacher took a bag of soybeans and scattered them throughout a peach orchard below the mountain. He then told the priest: "On the day that you have picked up all of these beans and refilled this bag, I will transmit the Dao to you."

This young Daoist priest then demonstrated great perseverance. He spent half a year picking up the soybeans. My teacher was very pleased and said to him: "Every morning, you must pick up all of the leaves that have fallen at the entrance of the courtyard here. Only then can you sit to meditate."

What this Daoist priest didn't know was that the leaves would fall endlessly down on the ground and there was no way to completely clean them up. This method was one of the ways certain masters chose to select students that year who were able to apply themselves.

In this day and age, for those who want to transmit and teach something, what they most fear is not finding a single person with perseverance. As a matter of fact, when it comes to studying the Dao, the most important part is having a mind that is relaxed, quiet, complete,[78] and stable.

---

77 求道 (*qiudao*). Either seeking teachings of Daoism from a master, seeking a direct experience of the truth that Daoism expounds or the path to that experience.

78 圆 (*yuan*). The mind when not ruffled or segmented by distracting or discursive thoughts.

The mind in a state of true rest is like a wild goose gliding silently over a pool, or like a boat drifting over a river, leaving no lines upon the water. Whether speaking, silent, moving, or still, the mind is at rest and peaceful. When a meditator's mind becomes truly still, they become like a person engulfed in a teeming crowd paying no attention to the turmoil of the mortal world—they stay untainted. It makes no difference whether they are moving or still. This is a state that can only be entered into when fully relaxed.

In the deepest states of stillness, the meditator would not so much as bat an eyelid if a swarm of flies buzzed past their ears. Even if 1,000 ants were to crawl over their body, they would remain unmoved, their mind as vast as the galaxies and free from any disturbance. The mind in this state abides in a singular, uniform stillness, otherwise known in Buddhism as the state of "suchness."[79] The utmost pinnacle of this state can be described as the emptiness of both the mind and the state itself. In the beginning stages of practice this state is attainable through sitting meditation. As you gradually deepen your practice of this state, you can reach the point where even subtle discursive thoughts do not arise as you go about various activities in your day, whether conversing, driving, eating, using the toilet, or even while sleeping.

True "completeness" surpasses even the state of xin zhai zuo wang[80] in that you go beyond just "forgetting" reputation, fortune, food, sleep, praise, criticism, success, and failure. Through the practice of the mind and maintaining stillness, you reach a level where you are immersed in the material world yet remain unmoved by what the eyes see, the ears hear, the nose smells, the tongue tastes, the body touches, and the mind thinks. It is

---

79   如如 (ruru). Ever aware of the constantly active mind stuff, the effect-producing cause.

80   心齋坐忘. Xin zhai is the pure mind—the mind must be in a state of emptiness in order for the Dao to appear. Zuo wang means to "sit and forget," or to forget the body, mind, and all things associated with the self in order to meld with the myriad things.

a state where your six roots and six dusts[81] no longer serve as obstructions. Notions such as "self and other," or "right and wrong," are completely powerless to disturb the mind. The mind is broad, open, clear, illuminated, and boundless. This is the ultimate relaxation, stillness, perfection, and settling, and it is only possible when one's meditation occurs seamlessly whether in motion or at rest. Only if you meditate to this level will you truly experience the complete transformation of yourself.

Everything within Daoist meditation and the greater path of the Dao is connected in some way to the flow of *yin* and *yang*. If the mind is unable to enter into a state of stillness, it will be impossible to find peace within yourself and you will become a receptacle for "impure" *qi*. This accumulation of impure *qi*, known also as "postnatal *qi*,"[82] is what bars access to the *qi* of your original nature. Dirty *qi* can be described as the "dust" of all mundane affairs, including sexual relations. The *qi* created through the path of immortality, also known as "the path of the Dao," can only develop in a state of stillness that comes from meditating until not one speck of mundane "dust" settles on the mind. Attaining this state will spark the circulation of our true *qi*.[83] This *qi* is activated and circulates without the aid of our intention—this is the movement of self-nature. At this time we gather the medicine,[84] a process which requires a qualified teacher's instructions on breathing and the *qi*'s circulatory pathways. Sometimes, for example, the *qi* needs to circulate in the reverse direction, or sometimes to be moved gently, or sometimes with force. The *sifu* will usually work closely

---

81 六根 (*liu gen*): 眼根 (*yan gen*), 耳根 (*er gen*), 鼻根 (*bi gen*), 舌根 (*she gen*), 身根 (*shen gen*), 意根 (*yi gen*) or "wu yan er bi she shen yi."
六塵 (*liu chen*): 色塵 (*se chen*), 聲塵 (*sheng chen*), 香塵 (*xiang chen*), 味塵 (*wei chen*), 觸塵 (*chu chen*), 法塵 (*fa chen*) or "se shen xiang wei chu fa."
The six roots refer to the six senses (the five primary senses and "thought" as the sixth); the dusts are the objects of those senses, or more specifically the qualities produced by those objects.

82 後天之氣 (*houtianzhiqi*). As opposed to prenatal *qi*, postnatal *qi* is considered "dirty" as it is acquired after birth.

83 真氣 (*zhenqi*). This is the healthy *qi* accumulated through practice, as opposed to "dirty" or "contaminated *qi*."

84 採藥 (*caiyao*). The process whereby *jing* (essence) and *qi* energy is moved from the *dantian* and accumulated in preparation for further practices.

with a student during this period of time and observe any changes to their physical and mental constitution. The process cannot be hurried, and ideally the guide should be proficient in the theory of energy channels and herbal prescriptions, should it be necessary.

If you don't have access to a qualified teacher, it's best not to dabble in the practices of the micro- and macrocosmic orbits, or the movement of the Celestial Chariot.[85] In my experience, this is the best way to avoid inflicting injury on yourself.

This method for sitting meditation is extremely simple and safe, and requires no knowledge of the divinatory symbols and trigrams. The only thing you have to do is breathe naturally while quieting the body and mind. You are completely absorbed in your environment, without becoming senseless and unaware. Bring your focus consistently to the breath as it goes in and out, and with time you will have unwittingly reached the level of turtle breathing. Some people will have certain experiences as they become proficient in this type of breathing. In the rarest of cases, they will suddenly be able to hear or see things hundreds of miles away, or experience the body twisting and bending like a kaleidoscope. The point in all of this is to keep to the principle of "thinking without thoughts" in order to keep yourself unattached and your focus fixed on the coming and going of your breath.

---

85 河車搬運 (hechebanyun). A practice of circulating *qi* through the governing and conception channels.

CHAPTER 29

HOW TO OVERCOME DESIRE

Men who reach this phase of their meditation might feel a sudden "sprouting" of the *yang qi*. Sitting with the heels of your feet pressed into the perineum acupoint can prevent the leakage of seminal fluids. Nonetheless, many men lose all of their progress and give up at this stage because their desire is so strong. When the *qi* begins to move, it triggers the release of rising *qi* in the *dantian*, causing erections. If you understand the body's cosmic orbits through which the *qi* circulates, you can potentially use this rising *qi* as a means to enhance your true *qi*.

Knowing how to take precautions against this kind of leakage and protecting your life essence are basic concepts a novice meditator should have. If a meditator can abide by these, he will have the further opportunity to transform his *qi* and spirit. It is quite normal for the average man to release seminal fluids. However, for those who practice Daoism and sitting meditation, this is not something to be taken lightly. To put it into perspective: it is said that one drop of semen is equivalent to 100 drops of blood; every measure should be taken to prevent any loss. In Daoism, sexual release can be attributed to a loose pubococcygeal (PC) muscle, which controls ejaculation. Steps must be taken to first "lay the foundation." In as little as 100 days, the depleted body can be restored.

The next step is for the essence (seminal fluid) to be transformed into true *qi*. Once the transformation is complete, leakages will not easily escape from the body. Having sporadic erections doesn't suggest "persistent energy arising;" it may just be a physical response. If you have truly experienced this "persistent energy arising," you must immediately concentrate on the energy. Furthermore, to even be considered for the stage of "gathering the medicine," there cannot be the slightest trace of lust, even in your dreams. Diligently practice until there's no leakage. A qualified teacher will be able to clarify if your rising *yang* energy is real or just a trick of the body, and whether you have advanced to the stage of gathering the medicine and are prepared for the practice of the cosmic orbits.

It is a common problem for many men to leak their male reproductive fluid. This problem is sometimes related to "insufficient kidney water"[86] and sometimes to over-thinking. At other times, the mind and body are completely worn out and exhausted, so it's easy for the fluid to leak, or for the fluid to mix with the urine. There was once a lay practitioner who would annually spend a month or two, during spring, in retreat on Qingcheng Mountain. Due to the aforementioned problem, he would experience many symptoms, such as dizziness, pale complexion, night sweats, and feeling cold in the lower back and knees, all of which would make sitting for long periods of time utterly impossible. When he would fall ill, it felt like there were pins and needles in his buttocks and lower back area, which prevented him from being able to walk. He asked my Daoist *sifu* about this. After *sifu* took his pulse, he asked him: "When you were young, did you masturbate a lot?" The practitioner could only smile in response. My master then taught him the secrets of how to strengthen his "renal function." The master grabbed a piece of white cloth, onto which he recited an incantation, tied a knot, and then handed it to the practitioner. The master then told him: "Never take this off, day or night." Strangely enough, this practitioner had no further recurring problems with male reproductive fluid leakage after that.

Sifu gave a different method to another lay practitioner. He gave him a prescription, telling him to purchase medicine from an herbalist in Chengdu, the city in which he resided. The practitioner took the medicine to gently nourish his kidneys in order to improve their function. Then he was told to put his focus on his *dantian* for 100 days while meditating from 5am to 7am and 11am to 1pm. This practitioner achieved the stage of "involuntary erection with

---

86 腎水不足 (*shenshuibuzu*). From Chinese Medicine, this refers to the reduced metabolism and endocrine function due to the poor nutrition and fluid control of our body.

the absence of desire." He asked how to proceed and was told: "This means you've restored your kidney function (or renal *qi*). Now when you have involuntary erections while meditating, stare directly at this point, lightly curl your tongue back, clench your teeth together, straighten your spine, and clench your jaw. You have been able to achieve spontaneous heat in the *dantian* within the space of 100 days! This may just be your karmic destiny! Not only that, but the intensity of the heat reached the point of burning off your belt. This proves you certainly have some past life connections to this practice. If this information was not told to you, you would have deviated from the path. If you have an involuntary erection, clench your teeth tightly, bring your tongue to the upper palate, make a slightly forceful inhalation, and hold your breath until you can't any longer. Put your focus on the perineal area, and the erection will slowly subside. This method can't be employed frequently, otherwise your organ will withdraw."

Sifu once reminded me that this method differs according to the constitution of each person's body, so it cannot be repeated verbatim to different people, otherwise it will cause confusion and disorder. The master must transmit this information personally and directly to the disciple in the absence of a third party. This method, in particular, cannot be done carelessly because it involves subtle adjustments to your practice, as well as following oral instructions on how to circulate *qi* in the body.

In particular, the method of gathering the medicine is by no means a trivial matter, as the actual "medicine" results from the transformation of our essence, *qi*, and spirit through ascetic practice. For the average person, if they cannot achieve a state in which their body and mind are free from desires, fantasies, and thoughts, from whence would there be any 'medicine' to collect? One must be especially careful here, as many people often mistake some physical changes caused by desires for the true *qi*. A practitioner must achieve a state free from the taints and bonds of all mundane hopes and desires. But out of millions of people, how many practitioners can actually do that? Therefore, in order to avoid negative consequences, the oral instructions and the practice of *qi* should not be indiscriminately revealed to others.

CHAPTER **30**

THE ROLE OF THE GOVERNING AND CONCEPTION CHANNELS IN MEDITATION

Sifu said: "Whether you use meditation as a means to cultivate your health or as a practice of spiritual cultivation, you will necessarily come across the conception and governing channels. From the perspective of *yin* and *yang*, the conception channel is classified as *yin* and the governing channel as *yang*. The conception channel starts at the teeth in the lower jaw and extends to the perineum. The governing channel starts at the perineum and extends to the teeth of the upper jaw. The conception channel goes downward, while the governing channel extends upward.

"According to the Daoist tradition, if through the practice of austerities you 'open up' these two channels, then you will have opened up the microcosmic orbit. If, beyond this, the *qixue* (*dantian*), *huangting* (around the center of the torso), and *niwan* (crown of the head) areas of the body can be opened as well, this is known as having 'opened' the 'macrocosmic orbit' (energy channels within the torso, head, arms, and legs).

"The conception and governing channels, along with the eight extraordinary channels,[87] are all linked. The eight extraordinary channels are composed of the conception, governing, *chong* (thrusting), and *dai* (girdling), channels as well as the *yangwei* channel (*yang* linking) which governs the outer surface of the body. There is also the *yinwei* channel (*yin* linking) governing the inner section of the body, the *yangqiao* channel (*yang* springing)

87　奇經八脈 (*qijingbamai*). A group of eight channels that have names but no points of their own. They relate to strengthen the connection between the other channels as well as store the fundamental substances (*qi*, blood, essence, etc.) of the body.

governing the *yang* section of the horizontal axis of the body, and the *yinqiao* channel (*yin* springing) governing the *yin* section of the horizontal axis of the body. Daoist books commonly refer to the microcosmic orbit as the movement of the Celestial Chariot. To put it more simply, it means the area beneath the lower lip, which in physiognomy is referred to as the *chengjiang* (sauce receptacle): from here, down to the perineum is the conception channel. Going back from the perineum, past the anus, following the sacrum, ascending to the top of the head, going down past the center of the eyebrows, tip of the nose and center of the upper lip (philtrum), before finally reaching the gums of the upper teeth, is the governing channel.

"In practicing the various meditation and breathing practices of the different schools, most practitioners will experience a rise in *yang qi*. Once the vital energy of the body starts moving, this *qi* will spread and ascend, gradually making its way up the spinal column. According to various oral tips from the masters of a number of schools, you can drive this *qi* with the breath and in this way move it up either side of the spine to the *yuzhen* ('jade pillow' point at the back of the head), then downward from the *baihui* (crown of the head) via the *shanggen* (top of the nose), and down beyond the nostrils (*lantai*: left nostril and the *tingwei*: right nostril). The *qi* then moves past the lips to the *chengjiang* (area under the lower lip). From there it continues via the *tanzhong* (chest center) through to the stomach and intestinal area, and after one loop it arrives at the *dantian*. Genuinely opening up the conception and governing channels is not achieved by means of intention or force. This *qi* movement arises from the practitioner being in a state of deep stillness, such that the movement of the Celestial Chariot happens absolutely spontaneously.

"Opening up the conception and governing channels (the microcosmic orbit) will be of great help in dealing with most congenital or acquired deficiencies or imbalances. Endocrine imbalances and dysfunctions spring from the aging of the pituitary glands. If you can 'open' your conception and governing channels through meditation practice, it will certainly change your constitution. It will directly benefit the nervous, endocrine, and hormonal systems. It can also rejuvenate you, restore youthful vigor, beautify your skin, and clear any obstructions of *qi* and blood circulation. Meditative practices to prevent the aging process are especially suitable for women concerned about menopause.

"The conception channel is also of huge benefit to the kidney *qi*. If meditation practice is done over a long time, men will not have any problems with the prostate gland, nor will women have problems in related areas. If after meditation, the palms are rubbed together until warm, and rubbed over the *dantian* in a circular motion 64 times—clockwise for men and counterclockwise for women—no matter whether you're male or female you will reap enormous benefits. This can stabilize your foundations and nurture your original *qi*. For both men and women it can guard against the aging process. For women this can prevent abnormal leukorrhea as well as uterine and ovarian diseases. For men it is effective in dealing with prostate problems, impotence, and deficiency of the kidneys. Following a meditation session with massage can also prevent insomnia. Opening the conception and governing channels will bring an end to sensations of cold in the hands or feet, and will resolve problems of the immune system. Indeed, the benefits are too many to be listed here."

CHAPTER 31

MOVING THE CELESTIAL CHARIOT

Insights from an Adept

When *sifu* had gotten to this point, he was careful to reiterate: "There are two different possible directions for the movement of energy along the conception and governing channels. In general they are both directed with intention and the support of the breath. When the conception channel is ready to move, upon inhalation lead the intention from the point between the eyebrows down to the *tanzhong* point at the center of the chest, in line with the nipples, and then straight down to the area of the *dantian*. Upon exhalation, following the same line, draw the intention back up to the point in the center of the chest. Generally speaking, if the *qi* is truly moving and the channel is opening, the feeling for the practitioner will be that of sitting in a hot spring in the winter, or of being slightly tipsy. Along with this will be the warm sensation of *qi* moving from the point in the center of the upper lip (*renzhong*) toward the *tanzhong*. The sensation will be like that of the palms of the hands being placed onto the surface of a boiling pot, not a normal kind of warmth at all. Sometimes there's also a general feeling of heat and at other times there isn't.

"You could even take it a step further at this point and inspect your saliva. Does your mouth fill up without needing to stir with the tongue? The saliva should be like the sweetness around the teeth and cheeks after consuming sugarcane, or it should be like the aftertaste from longanberry juice. Furthermore, the sweetness flows unceasingly. For certain practitioners with a good foundation this will eventually lead to the opening of the governing channel.

"Most beginner students will have to take it slowly, step by step. Using intention to guide the *qi* will take some time and the *dantian* area of the belly will slowly develop the sensation of warmth.

Generally, when the *dantian* begins to feel warm then the center of the chest, the belly, arms, and hands will become warm as well. Practice in this way, moving the *qi* up and down, inhaling and exhaling. You just need to remember that when you inhale the *qi* must move down, and upon exhaling it must rise back up to the *tanzhong* point in the center of the chest. This *qi* will fill the throat, and the whole lower jaw including the teeth.

"Some people are in a rush and feel warmth in the *dantian* area, waist, and upper body, including the arms down to the ten fingertips. But often this is just a sensation in the body and not an authentic opening of the conception channel. The real opening of the conception channel involves a very clear sensation of *qi* moving through the body at a deeper level, so therefore the feeling of heat is also at a deeper level. It's not just a feeling of warmth on the surface of the skin. This point needs to be given special attention.

"At this time, a teacher with clear understanding will give the student oral tips to guide the *qi* downward. If the downward moving *qi* has not started, then complications can easily arise when going a step further and opening the governing channel. If too little experience has been accumulated, or the opening of the channel is a false one, sometimes a blockage of the *qi* in the lower body will cause sensations of tenderness, soreness, or numbness. At this time you may need to rely on treatment with moxibustion, incense, and complementary Chinese Medicine, combined with certain physical practices in order to open the channel.

"According to what most experienced practitioners say, if the downward moving *qi* is not flowing through and the governing channel is practiced, then there will be some negative results. When *qi* and blood are really understood, then deliberate guidance along the bone marrow and blood vessels won't be needed. There will be a rapid flow of heat moving from the tailbone straight to the top of the head, and then from the top of the head back down again. If movement in this direction is unhindered, then of course movement in the reverse direction will not be a problem.

"It must be remembered that the reverse movement is from the *dantian* upward, past the nose, the top of the head, the back of the head, and then along the spine all the way down to where the perineum connects with the conception channel. The movement is then repeated in this way continuously.

"When practicing the movement of the Celestial Chariot, chronic illnesses might flare up again. If so, at that time one must consult an experienced practitioner. This is because of the path that the *qi* takes: from the *dantian*, past the sacrum, up the spine, past the back of the head, past the top of the head, between the eyebrows, past the nose, through the mouth and throat, and through the center of the chest. These are very sensitive areas of the body, full of important nerves and the greatest massing of glands including the pituitary. For some with a weaker constitution, in the early stages of the practice some childhood illnesses that may still be residing in the body could come out. But with patience, once you open the microcosmic orbit, the body will heal itself. For some, whether it's owing to improved strength, physical energy, or complexion, there will be the clear appearance of rejuvenation."

CHAPTER 32

WHEN YOU CAN'T SIT STILL, COOL THE FIRE IN YOUR HEART

When *sifu* would reach a certain point in his instruction, he would venture to share some of his personal experience and insights regarding sitting meditation. When young and training in the mountains, he had gotten to know many of the Daoist priests living there. The older priests in particular thought well of him for regularly lending a hand to many of the temple tasks such as acting as scribe, making handwritten copies of the sacred texts, or running down the mountain to buy supplies and other necessities. It was in this way that he also procured the stories of their experiences on the path of practice.

Sifu once gave me a meditation tip for dealing with a sudden rush of unstoppable thoughts or turbulent emotions. "If the onset is strong enough to keep you from remaining seated," he said, "you should take time to physically and mentally relax. Go for a short walk. When you come back, rub your hands together until warm and massage your *yongquan* points on the bottoms of your feet until they also warm up. Next, move your eyes up and down, left and right and then revolve them 360 degrees. Finish by forcefully closing and opening the eyes a few times. The last exercise is, while posting, to lift the heels up and then drop down with force, followed by lightly patting and rubbing the inner thighs and working out toward the rest of the legs. You can wrap up by walking in place before returning to meditation. You will find that these methods help to reduce scattered thoughts and afflictions."

Sifu also added in a bit more information for dealing with the mind when it's frenetic and unsettled (like when you know something is about to happen and you can't sit still, or if your chest area feels agitated and uncomfortable). To deal with this excess "heart fire,"[88] you can use the method of concentrating on certain focal points inside and outside the body. Focus your eyes lightly on the *shanggen* (top of the nose) and take three to seven breaths before moving your focus to the spot approximately 4½ fingers width below the belly button. Your mind will gradually become calm and settled again.

---

88   心火 (*xinhuo*). A Chinese Medicine term referring to an excess of heat in the heart system (not to be confused with the actual heart organ). This can disrupt the heart and cause insomnia, inability to focus, irritability, etc.

CHAPTER **33**

SAFE MEDITATION AND THE BATHING PRACTICE

Sifu said that when he was young, he met an old practitioner from the Macau Tung Sin Tong Charitable Society. This practitioner taught him a few fundamental methods for meditation practice. My teacher told me: "In the future, if you meet with younger people who are interested in meditation, yet it's not convenient to immediately transmit oral tips, then you can teach them this. It's the safest meditation technique." He instructed me to take notes.

This was the first time I was allowed to take notes. Direct memorization was always the standard for practice methods or oral tips; this is how it was during the course of my teacher's studies on the mountain as well. In his time it wasn't quite so convenient—notes would have been taken with a writing brush. In my case, we were required to simply remember what we were told. Only then could it be said that it was truly ours. So this is a habit that I've had since I was young and it would be difficult to change. However, on that occasion I was given permission to take notes, so I very quickly found a notebook and a ballpoint pen.

The following is what I recorded: "There are a great number of meditation techniques taught by various schools: over 100 techniques. The most reliable method without too many requirements is to sit in the 'double lotus' posture. The method is very simple. All that is required is a meditation cushion 3–5-centimetres high. The height can be adjusted according to the needs of the person. This raised posture helps support the body and focus the mind. In addition, the body needs to be completely relaxed, particularly the muscles. If the muscles are too tense, then mental tranquility may be harder to achieve. Place the hands in the *samadhi mudra*. This means the hands are placed in the lap, below the *dantian*, with the palms facing upward. One hand is laid above the other, with the thumbs gently touching. For men, the left hand should be on top; for women, the right. This position will help the circulation of blood and *qi*, keeping them unobstructed for the duration of the practice. This posture is very much like creating a connection to unite and harmonize the polarities of *yin* and *yang*, as in the taiji.

"When meditating, the chest and back, stomach and waist must all be straight. The abdomen and *dantian* should be drawn in but without slouching. The anus should be slightly contracted, but not forcefully because this could result in excessive heat[89] in the body, as well as hemorrhoids. The shoulders must be relaxed and even. Don't lean to either side or sway forward or back. The chest should not be lifted, but relaxed and open. This will allow the breathing to be smooth and unhindered, the idea being that the breath should be able to move freely. The head should be straight and the chin tucked in slightly. A smile will relax the nerves of the face. Place the tongue on the roof of the mouth. The eyes should be half opened. Fully opened eyes will be too stimulating for the mind and will hinder concentration, whereas if the eyes are closed it will be easy to doze off. Focus the eyes on a point in front with the help of the breath. This should be enough."

These were all points told to me by my teacher—a concise outline of what a modern individual would need to meditate. Of course, my teacher explained very clearly the reason for these essential points. When a truly sincere person, willing to commit long periods of time to practice, comes along, it is necessary to explain the details of each of these movements, including the physiological implications.

At that time, *sifu* kindly continued to instruct, giving a further account of his time on Qingcheng Mountain, where he had met a fellow practitioner named Yuanyin, who taught him the "*qi* bathing practice." *Sifu* said: "You can apply these movements as self-massage when you exit your meditation. It will be beneficial to your blood and *qi* circulation, and will prevent any stagnation of

---

89   上火 (*shanghuo*). In Chinese Medicine, if there is too much heat that develops in the body, illness can result.

these from sitting for long periods. This also activates the cells of the body and promotes youthfulness. Many wonderful things can result from this practice."

CHAPTER 34

THE LINK BETWEEN THE MEDITATIONS OF THE QINGCHENG AND WENSHI SECTS

I once found a Daoist book on a book stand. The cover showed a series of pictures delineating the origin and development of various Daoist sects. Having read this book, I was moved by curiosity to "trace the river back to its source." One weekend, I used the time when *sifu* had just finished eating his lunch to respectfully make an inquiry: "Could I please ask *sifu* to tell me about the origin and lineage of his Daoist school?" *Sifu* nodded his head and said: "This I should indeed tell you. This question has crossed my mind before, and I had originally planned to tell you all of this in the course of your study as the opportunities presented themselves. Seeing as you have brought it up now, I will give you a brief explanation. However, the lineage character code can only be found on the booklet you receive upon taking oaths in the order, and it is not permitted to divulge this information to anyone other than the disciples of one's own sect. As for me, in my 17th year, I paid homage in succession to three Daoist priests who would later become my teachers, two of whom belonged to the Qingcheng Sect. The other belonged to the Wenshi Sect, which started with Daozu and was transmitted to the elder Chen Tuan, who then passed it to the sage Huolong, who then gave it to Zhang Sanfeng, and so on in a single line all the way to Huang Yuanji."

When *sifu* reached this point, he specifically mentioned the books written by Huang Yuanji as worthy of consultation. In those days, if you were taken as a student of the "Path of Immortals," you would almost certainly have come across his books. In particular the *Le Yu Tang Yulu*[90] (a compilation of notes on Daoist teachings) and *Daomen Yuyao*[91] (a Qing dynasty book related to internal alchemy), which can still be found on book stands up to this day. *Sifu* said: "In those years I spent up in the mountains, I received the *Xuanzong Koujue*[92] (mysterious and profound oral tips) and *Xinjing Zhujie*[93] (*Annotations to the Heart Sutra*) from my master's very own hands, and he made a point of telling me that it was meant only for me to copy and should not be lent to anyone else. In them can be found a great number of very important oral tips of enormous benefit to anyone practicing Daoism and cultivating the *dantian*. In the Wenshi School, the focal point is on the last stage of 'refining the spirit and returning to emptiness.' It abides by the tenets of the joint practice of body and mind. However, spiritual cultivation is the directing factor. It emphasizes 'non-attachment' to extreme outer or inner stillness and emptiness, and even non-attachment to the idea of non-attachment itself, so as to experience the 'extreme of no-extreme and achieve pure *yang qi*.'"

At this point *sifu* added: "Do you remember at the very onset of your meditation practice when I told you to memorize the 5,000 character version of the *Dao De Jing*[94] within one week? Now, I can tell you that the main reason for this was that someday in the future, when you reach the stage of 'refining essence into *qi*, refining *qi* into spirit, and refining spirit to return to emptiness,' you can refer back to the *Wenshi Scripture*, the *Yin Mark Scripture* and the *Dao De Jing*. In this way, you can understand which of the states of *dantian* cultivation are true and which are false, as well as become familiar with the subtleties of 'emptiness.' The hardest aspect of meditation is that you need to sit until you forget all about your spirit; if you are still attached to the spirit, there is no way you can enter the state of utmost stillness and emptiness. This makes it very hard to go one step further and return to emptiness; and without this the meditative state that one can achieve is just

---

90 樂育堂語錄.

91 道門語要.

92 玄宗口訣.

93 心經註解.

94 道德經. A fundamental text to both religious and philosophical Daoism from the 6th century credited to Laozi.

not comparable, which is a great pity. At this point in time you probably don't understand what I'm telling you, but be sure to remember every word. One day it will make sense."

Actually, the Mount Qingcheng lineage is a branch of the Longmen School. *Sifu* said: "The master I followed back in those days could be regarded as a leader of the renaissance of the Longmen School (the Wang Changyue system).[95] He was reportedly an inheritor of the teachings of Master Yanxia from the Longmen School. At that time, when one received their precepts, one knew very clearly to which generation one belonged. However, if you were to analyse things a little more closely, you would see that the main point of the practice methods of the Longmen School also come from Daozu's recommendation as taking the state of *xu ji jing du*[96] as the goal and from there moving to the ultimate state of *ling ming miao hua*.[97] If in the course of our meditation we can have our mind enter a state like a great waveless ocean and a dustless universe, as time goes by our *yang qi* will of itself become exuberant, and in the fullness of time, the true *qi* will arise of itself. The most important spiritual cultivation method of the Qingcheng lineage is to use the healthy *qi* of heaven and earth in order to expel and replace any negative *qi* we may have acquired. This is combined with the oral tips for cultivating a mind free of distracting thoughts and delusion, until ultimately one is completely indivisible from heaven and earth. You just need to remember that by attaining your true pure, original essence and spirit, you can prolong your life. Only if you avoid getting lost and bogged down in the pleasure of the 'original essence and spirit' will you be able to reach the fulfillment of 'refining the spirit and returning to emptiness.' This is the most important oral tip to attaining the highest fruit of immortality. Bear this in mind! Bear this in mind!"

Whenever I have a small accomplishment in meditation, I feel tremendous and fervent gratitude for *sifu*'s benevolence. Today, as I think back on this, if I have any small insight to share with others

---

95 王常月的系統. Dragon Gate School, Master Wang Changyue's lineage.

96 虛極靜篤. From the *Dao De Jing*, Ch 16: "Let emptiness fill you. Let stillness reign within."

97 靈明妙化. A high meditative state.

this is all due to *sifu*'s earnest exhortations, and it was under his tireless instruction that I was able to receive whatever insights I have. Although *sifu* has long passed on, every time I sit down to meditate it's as if his measureless blessings sweep over me like the spring breeze.

CHAPTER 35

TOTAL FOCUS ON THE BREATH UNITING MIND AND *QI*

At one point I came to a juncture while meditating, and later consequently seized an opportune moment to ask *sifu* for instructions: "*Sifu* has in the past taught me how to regulate my breath, but often, when I focus with rapt attention on a certain cavity I feel unsure."

Following this, *sifu* offered a clearer explanation on several points: "There is an important point to consider when meditating, when you have regulated your breath to a comfortable state, to the point of being barely discernible, and your mind is in a state of extreme relaxation, then your breath can come in and out freely. The main point lies in the entry and exit of the breath: On your inhalations and exhalations you must use your mind to silently accompany the breath. At the same time, remember, the mind focused entirely on the breath is what we call the 'seat of rapt attention.'" Very clearly, *sifu* simultaneously guided my attention with his finger toward each acupoint and explained the particular method of "guarding" it.

After hearing this explanation, I suddenly felt like everything had opened up and become crystal clear. Sifu went one step further and very compassionately continued his explanation, saying emphatically: "In meditation and the regulation of one's breath, one must also understand the *zi* period (from 11pm to 1am) and the *wu* period (from 11am to 1pm), as well as other optimal times for the flow of certain channels. The human breath is divided into flourishing, assisted, dead, resting, and imprisoned. The period before noon is prime time to develop your *qi* through meditation, although the absolute best times are during the *zi* and *wu* periods. It is best if the methods and times for meditative practice can be transmitted to you via an experienced teacher.

"When you breathe in, count down in your mind from 10 to 1 and then keep the breath in for the same amount of time before slowly letting the breath out so finely that you yourself cannot hear its sound. If over time, your inhalations become longer, and your exhalations become shorter, then you can keep practicing until the breath naturally comes to an abrupt stop. You can stick a piece of cotton paper between your upper lip and nostrils to confirm. Eventually you can reach the point where your breathing comes not through the mouth or nose but 'internally', in much the same manner as a fetus breathes in the mother's womb. At this point you will clearly sense a portion of the breath quivering around the *dantian*. At that time, the piece of paper under your nostrils will be absolutely still, which signifies that you have already grasped the method of 'turtle breathing', and the only question then is how long you can hold it for. Some can take one breath and then they won't need to breathe again for the rest of the day. Some teachers will observe their student's condition, and at this stage they may tell the students how to activate their original *qi* (through the practice of 'gathering medicine'). This process is not guided by forced thinking; if so, then what is achieved cannot be categorised as real fetal breathing. When going into a fetal breathing state you will feel that the external world is like a mirage, like an illusory fairyland of little substance; however, your mind will be in a state of absolute clear understanding.

"What's important here is that your focus and energy should be placed wholly on the breath. When you focus, there must be no delusive or distracting thoughts. Any such thoughts will mean you cannot collect your *qi* at any given acupoint. The explanations of this particular point vary slightly across the different schools, but in any case you must receive this teaching from a qualified teacher. Do not try this on your own. You musn't practice blindly."

What *sifu* was pointing to is that, when circulating the *qi* toward the *dantian*, the mind and breath are interwoven and focused on the *dantian* to the point where the original *qi* arises. One thus meditates in a natural and thoughtless state, free from distraction or interference, the mind at one with heaven and earth, until even the breath is no longer! When the *qi* and spirit unite, the *yang qi* will spontaneously arise.

Sifu continued: "This isn't so easy. Most people who meditate up to this point will misunderstand some aspect of their experience. In summary, one must make the mind return to the state it experienced while in the mother's womb, free from any desire and complicated thoughts. Nor is there any breathing through the mouth or nose—all the *qi* enters through the navel. This is in fact the fundamental principle of 'turtle breathing.' When you genuinely experience turtle breathing, you will very distinctly feel a portion of *qi* lingering and buzzing around the *dantian*. This shows that you have truly grasped turtle breathing. I usually recommend that people do their best to avoid 'guarding' acupoints, because if the method is incorrect it can cause swelling. Therefore it is best to avoid 'guarding' them altogether. Although you might at times feel unclear and lack a central focus, if you persevere you will in the end achieve results."

CHAPTER 36

STUDYING WITH ELDERS OF VARIOUS SCHOOLS

Generally speaking, there are over a dozen acupoints that Daoist practitioners will "guard." One day *sifu* said: "Once, atop a mountain, a ceremony of fasting in worship of the sky was held,[98] and among the Daoist priests in attendance, there was a particular elder whose fontanelle, or the crown of his head, would at times swell when he chanted [the liturgies]. At other times it would cave in slightly. Furthermore, his voice wasn't really emitted from his mouth, which astonished all those in attendance. When the ceremony finished one week later, I approached this elder out of curiosity and we had a talk. He told me: 'In days gone by when I wandered to Xikang, I met a Lama who transmitted some *Vajrayana* yoga[99] recitation methods to me. He also imparted the grand empowerments of *dumo*[100] and *phowa*.[101] From doing the recitations I gradually came to comprehend *qi* for myself, and as a result of this I practiced a blend of these methods and the fetal breathing of Daoism. From time to time, I naturally breathe without the air passing through the mouth or nose. Not a bit of what I am telling you is untrue.' This foreign elder also once told us that when he was about 70 years of age, his master told him to guard the acupoints, not focusing on his body but rather to fix

---

98 齋天儀式法會 (*zhaitianyishifahui*). Fasting ceremonies are a type of Daoist funeral ceremony. This particular one is referred to as a "heavenly fasting" ceremony.

99 金剛瑜伽 (*jingangyujia*). *Vajrayana* is one type (vehicle) of Buddhism that developed in northern India and Tibet. The other major vehicles of Buddhism are *Hinayana* and *Mahayana*.

100 拙火 (*zhuohuo*). *Vajrayana* Buddhist meditative practice. It refers to developing an "inner heat or fire" in the body.

101 頗瓦法 (*powafa*) Vajrayana Buddhist meditation practice. It may be described as the "transference of consciousness at the time of death."

his intention on the space about a fist's distance above the *baihui* (crown of the head). At times, he would instruct him to focus his attention about a fist's distance in front of the point where the eyes and top of the nose meet, or to 'guard' the point about 4½ fingers width below the navel. His master told him that his constitution was not suitable for guarding acupoints inside his body and that he should therefore guard the outside. From then on, he had continued in this way for close to 20 years, at all times and in all places in a state of unified mind and *qi*. We can really see just how numerous the practice methods within Daoism are."

All Daoist masters have their own particular ways to instruct their disciples. Another Daoist master of mine lived in Xizhi (an area of Taiwan) in a temple that his disciples had jointly built for him. It had four levels and the top one was where he went into retreat annually to practice immortality methods. Many were the times when I sat at his feet to beseech him for instruction on Daoist practice methods. Although I never took refuge in him formally as a disciple, he treated me in much the same way as if I had; I learned closely under him, and he was truly of great benefit to me.

During that period, I would often spend time with an older fellow practitioner. He originally was a teacher of the doctrine in the Yi Guan Dao[102] (a religious order). However, from childhood he had a preference for the path of cultivation of immortality, which he practiced diligently. He would regularly have dealings with Daoist priests who had come over to Taiwan from mainland China and who had similar spiritual ambitions to his own. He would often go and respectfully meet with people of high standing and, to the best of my knowledge, had met with over 100 such individuals. During a summer break in my third year of junior high school, he took me along to go and pay our respects to a few venerable elders. One such individual was a Daoist priest named Li, who resided in a National Taiwan University dormitory and who was then around 70 years old! I received many teachings in that place. Also, there was a certain teacher named Wang who lived in

---

102 一貫道. "The Consistent Way": A religious order that combines elements of Buddhism and Daoism. The movement flourished in the late Qing dynasty in Mainland China and is now prevalent in Hong Kong and Taiwan.

the Xindian district of Taipei. He was able to popularize the study
of the "Path of Immortals," and although very advanced in years,
he remained able to very naturally live in accordance with the Dao.
At that time already, my fellow practitioner assured me that this
teacher had long since attained the fruits of his practice. Although
over 80 years of age, to the eye he seemed 50 at most—a testimony
to the refinement and depth of his cultivation. There was also a
teacher named Sun, who for a long time unremittingly promoted
the Wang method of posting (a standing exercise) and shared his
family lineage of *Yijin Jing*.[103] He also shared other practices that
were not transmitted as part of a lineage and which benefited me
greatly. In the Wanhua district lived a certain elder named Xu. To
this day I feel deeply grateful for his tireless zeal in teaching, and
the painstaking care he took in providing explanations concerning
the practice of Daoist internal alchemy, making the complex
accessible. In brief, from the age of about 15 onward, I received
instructions from over ten highly accomplished Daoist priests.
And it was all thanks to the help of my fellow practitioner. Many
of these virtuous elders are now departing this world one after the
other, and I am left with a pang of shame at my lack of achievement.

---

103 易筋經. A Daoist *qigong* method which can be translated as the "Tendon
   Transformation Method."

CHAPTER **37**

A FORTUITOUS ENCOUNTER ONE WOULD NOT FORGET IN A LIFETIME

Previously, I mentioned the Daoist master's residence in Xizhi. The building was on a hill and initially an older cousin of mine had taken me there. This Daoist priest seemed to be middle-aged, and bore an air of refined grace and had something rather magical about his person. Only later after our discussion did I find out that he was already 80 years old. At the time of our visit, we also had a middle-aged companion with us, and if I recall correctly we discussed the concept of *xuan guan yi qiao*.[104]

Our companion respectfully addressed the elder: "*Sifu*, please may I ask a question? However much I seek to understand Lu Dongbin's *Hundred Character Stone Tablet*,[105] 'Whether in stillness or movement you know the origin, having achieved this, what more is there to seek?',[106] the meaning still eludes me. Would *sifu* be able to help me understand?"

Without a moment's hesitation the elder responded with an unceasing torrent of words that flowed like the Yangtze River: "This tells us that in every time and place we cannot allow our spirit to wander off. Our eyes, ears, and nose must all be under the governance of the mind, in order to cultivate *qi*. At the same time we must maintain one-pointed focus and have the mind tend toward tranquil stillness. Yet, by no means repress or force it. The only way is to be at ease and go with the flow of circumstances and to have the mind and *qi* work in concordance. Start cultivation and practice from peaceful tranquility.

---

104 玄關一竅. The concept of a "gate" allowing transfer of energy between a postnatal state and a primordial state.
105 百字碑 (*Baizibei*).
106 動靜知宗祖, 無事更尋誰 (*dongjingzhizongzu, wushigengxunshei*). *Baizibei*.

"Gradually, as you apply this to your everyday life, whether in movement or stillness and whether sitting or lying, all the while you will be self-possessed with your spirit unaffected by outside influences. At all times you will be able to maintain focus and attentiveness. If you can achieve this, however chaotic or clamorous your outer environment, your mind will not be disturbed."

This elder Daoist priest elaborated further for us three novices by mentioning recent developments in his practice: "To this day, I still practice seated meditation at least three times a day. In more busy times, I accordingly bring this focused, settled, and thoughtless state into my activity, and thus meld with all states. Throughout the day, whether I am imparting the doctrine, teaching, or chatting, I remain in a state akin to being alone, my mind a deep, waveless pool; and no matter the multifarious states that may arise, they depart without leaving a trace on the water."

When my cousin and I had entered the building and were waiting to be called upon by the elder, some of his students steeped some tea for us to drink. The location was remote and peaceful. Although it was not easy to get to, as you walked toward the elder's retreat centre, going up along stone steps on the side of the hill, you could see the sparkle and glitter of thousands of household lanterns lighting up the early evening. The temple had no border on any side and seemed to meld with the mountain. Although it was built on the top of a hill no more than 300 meters high, as one stood there and looked down, one nevertheless had a feeling of remoteness and solitude, of having left the world behind. We ascended the flights of stairs in light steps, towered over on either side by pine trees. Throughout the climb, the mind followed along one's steps unwittingly, itself ascending to a higher, more dignified state.

There was an open concrete area in front of the temple with a basketball court and badminton court. By strolling along a red-brick trail that ran between the two courts, we soon arrived at the entrance where two students very politely bowed with hands joined and welcomed us inside. My cousin and I both harboured a long-term infatuation with books and relished the feeling of being in a well-stocked library. As we walked in further and raised our eyes, we saw that the entire wall was covered in bookcases. My spirits were further raised by the faint smell of books that floated about the room, and my cousin cast me a glance to say: "Looks like we didn't come for nothing!"

After about ten minutes of sitting there, a female student came down to inform us that we could make our way upstairs to meet with the elder. As we walked up the stairs, we could see on our right side a Buddhist hall for worship that contained towering statues of the Three Pure Ones (three deities within Daoism), as well as a stately altar. Once we had ascended to the fourth floor (the roof of the main building), a traditionally styled building of red brick with a yellow, glazed tile roof appeared in front of us. One's eyes immediately caught the high, elegant bamboo that bordered the house. Unwittingly, I was completely absorbed into the simple and unadorned surroundings, as if I suddenly found myself standing inside an ancient painting.

We stepped into the elder gentleman's parlor. On the left was a visitors' area of a little less than 20 square meters where a long sofa and tea table had been arranged. The three of us waited there for a while as there were already others inside who were respectfully seeking guidance and instruction on the Dao from the master. From where we sat, we could vaguely hear the elder speaking in a composed manner, sounding disciplined and self-assured. Although at that time I was not so clear about the grandness and brilliance of this gentleman, I nonetheless listened with great joy. After about ten minutes, a group of men and women, seven or eight in number, walked out of the master's private room one by one.

As the three of us walked into his room, the man greeted us with great candor and a loud and resounding voice. Although he had seen his fair share of years, the white of his eyes was a light purple, like those of a child, and he was of a rosy complexion. What struck me were the peculiarly long tufts of "old-age" hairs growing from his ears down to his earlobes. I remembered from my study of physiognomy that this indicated powerful kidney qi, an uncommon vigor, and a sign of longevity. He courteously invited us to sit down on round, coffee-colored mats. When he himself was seated, he invited us to raise any questions we might have concerning practice and promised to do his utmost to answer our queries as best he could.

CHAPTER 38

UNATTACHED TO NAMES AND FORMS, THE THINGS OF THE WORLD ARE LIKE THE MOON REFLECTED IN WATER

My cousin started by asking the teacher about the most basic concept of refining essence into *qi*. The teacher compassionately explained in great detail the process of practice, starting from how to nurture *yang qi* and how to give rise to *yang qi* before then explaining how to "harvest" *yang qi*. The explanation went from the stage of guarding the lower *dantian* to the stage of starting to emit warmth from the *dantian*, and covered how to first increase the *dantian*'s original *qi* and then, once the *dantian* is filled with *yang qi*, how to coordinate the breath as well. The teacher said: "When you first start to practice, on every inhalation lightly take a slight portion of the breath into the *dantian* and use your intention to slightly lift the rectum; however, this is done without force. When you first start breathing in, you can try to hold the breath. Count from 1 to 10 and then exhale from the nostrils noiselessly and so softly that you do not feel it. Practice this repeatedly, gradually extending the time. What you must remember though, is to do this in a relaxed manner without force. Everyone must adjust the time in accordance with the length and intensity of their breath. Never hold your breath past your capacity as this could cause problems. Additionally, it's much safer to have a teacher who understands your physical and psychological state to guide you through this practice."

My cousin followed up with another inquiry: "Is there a simple and easy-to-learn method for fetal breathing?" The elder said to him: "Many are those who become perplexed by the piles of terms presented by Daoism. What is this 'gathering the medicine'? And what is this 'great medicine'? And this 'small medicine'? What about this 'inner medicine'? This 'outer medicine'? What is this 'true lead'? This 'mercury'? What are 'guarding the acupoints,' the 'yellow matron,' the 'cauldron,' the 'Taiyu goddess,' the 'martial fire,' the 'gentle fire,' the 'five vital breaths oriented to the origin,' and so on and so forth. None of these is what really matters. All the great adepts of the past loved to 'keep a hand up their sleeve' and thus used some confusing terms, so much so that one would be at a loss to know where to get started; some would go so far as to swap the front and back of a book, or take out and conceal a part of the oral tips it contains. These are all selfish ways of thinking. Of course, another reason for this is that one needs the guidance of a master to point out one's destiny so as to avoid going off track by groping blindly with wrong methods of practice.

"To put 'fetal breathing' simply, imagine that you are still a fetus, depending on your mother's amniotic fluid and breath. When your mother inhales, so do you; and the same goes for when she exhales. This is what we call 'same body breathing.' Thus, if you breathe in the appropriate way, you can naturally enter 'a state' such as the infant's. So, the *zhuan qi zhi rou, neng ying er hu*[107] which Laozi spoke of is a central point. Through cultivation of the breath in such a way over a period of time, your breath will in the end reach a stage where your inhalations and exhalations reach their final last point, your breath is as soft as silk, and your *qi* is like gossamer, uninterrupted and fine as if non-existent. Then you can naturally return to the state of a baby before the severing of the umbilical cord. In your daily life, waste less *qi*: fewer nerve-racking sights for the eyes, less decadent music entering your ears, no meaningless language from the mouth, and an end to all the thoughts in your mind. *Yi ling du cun*,[108] of which Zhang Sanfeng spoke, explains to us that dealing with the comings and goings in our daily life should be like reflections in a mirror: When things arise, we face them; and when they pass, they leave no trace of their passage. With an absence of any and all differentiation, one's real nature will

---

107 氣致柔, 能嬰兒乎. *Dao De Jing*, Chapter 10: "Focusing your *qi* within, be soft as a newborn."

108 一靈獨存. A state where only the enlightened mind exists.

be constantly present; and from dawn to dusk outside conditions cannot, even in the slightest way, unsettle the mind. Don't look down on these practices, even if they might not be immediately achievable for a practitioner."

The elder stated yet another example: "In Jilong, there was an old Daoist priest from the mainland whose cultivation was outstanding. It was said that he had already practiced to the stage of being able to retract his genitals. I don't know how this came about, but through one of his disciples he met a young Minnanese lady, 40 years his junior. Later on, after the lady had become his wife, she took all his savings and valuables and sold them. A short while after that, this old priest went crazy. His speech was deranged and he was in a completely dejected, down-and-out state. It was a sad sight indeed! A few of us fellow practitioners called upon him many times and supported him for a time."

Once the elder had spoken up to this point, he followed up by sharing with us young folk words of the elder Lu Chunyang: "Loads of gold and silver enough to fill a valley; the immortal sneers and disregards." Mencius and Confucius both spent their lives roaming, studying and teaching in various countries and enjoyed at times state sponsorship, but whether they were in favor or dire straits, they naturally carried on in the same way. While the elder Qiu Changchun cultivated the "Way," he was destitute to the point that he had not so much as a handful of rice to fill his stomach, yet his perseverance in practice remained constant throughout, and finally he awakened to the Dao. Later, he received the favor of the emperor of the Yuan dynasty, who took refuge in him. This emperor told him: "From this day onward, all of the temples, shrines and monasteries of the famous mountains of China are under your jurisdiction."

This caused no pride to swell in Changchun's heart. On the contrary, all the proceeds he collected went toward the construction and renovation of Daoist temples and the flourishing of his school. These examples show us that if the manner in which a practitioner regards and relates to wealth, companions, practice methods, and land is inappropriate, and if their thinking is not pure, then they may be tested by their demons.

Chapter **39**

Take Advantage of the Best Time for Practice

"As of now, you are all still quite young and there is still a long road ahead; there are many things yet to face. Our forefathers made careful and accurate notes of 30 kinds of obstacles that you will meet with in your practice. You should all study these thoroughly. Don't just busy yourself with the practice of inner alchemy. There are many opinions about the path, especially concerning *xuan guan yi qiao* (the concept of a 'gate' allowing transfer of energy between a postnatal state and a primordial state). You could say that we have a good karmic connection, so I can mention a few important concepts here. The reason this 'gate' is so mysterious and profound is that it doesn't exist within the body or any other specific location. It is neither inside nor outside. It requires that you have already realized the combination of essence and *qi*. Otherwise, you will have to acquire this. So, I recommend that you don't waste your time in studying [the wrong things].

"You have the fortune of practicing hard in your youth. I am sincerely happy for you. At your age, I didn't have the good fortune to encounter the guidance of a teacher. Perhaps this is a result of your own good connection to Daoism. You need to make the most of this precious human life. I will now take the initiative by telling you a few things you may experience in your day-to-day life, as well as some safe tips. What do you say?"

When this senior practitioner spoke these words, he looked at me with eyes full of kindness. To suddenly get special attention in this way caught me by surprise. At that time I was still quite young with little real-life experience so I felt slightly embarrassed and at a loss for a suitable response. Nevertheless I proceeded with a deep bow, with hands pressed together, and said: "Thank you very much, teacher."

The old man regarded me with a smile and a nod and began to relate: "At your age it's just about safe to assume that you are still a virgin, and relatively untainted by the bad habits of this world. You also haven't yet built up too many worldly hindrances. This really is an excellent time to practice.

"Every day, regardless of time or place, gently place your intention on the point 4½ fingers' width below the belly button; and when you find the spot, then bring your awareness in past the muscles by about 3–4 centimeters. The awareness is not placed on the surface or on the muscles but on a deeper level. Whenever you have time, put your attention there. Every day, if you get the chance to meditate put your attention here. As time passes, due to the depth of your concentration, your *qi* will unify. When your skill develops, your water element (*kan*) will naturally become pure; your essence, *qi*, and spirit will naturally return to their original position and coalesce into one. Most people sit for a long time without achieving, so they lose sight of what is most important. This practice is something that we can accomplish in our daily life. Whether or not the water and fire elements in your body are balanced will be determined by the balance between the heart and the kidney.

"People of today, even from childhood, are overrun by an onslaught of wild and fantastic thoughts. It has already become a habit and is very difficult to stop. Once we sit in meditation, and the body and senses no longer divert our attention, the myriad delusive thoughts grow like wildfire. According to the Daoist perspective, this is the rising of fire within the body. The lower body becomes weak and the circulation becomes obstructed. If someone is heavy or brooding with thoughts as they sit, their face will flush. Be very careful with this, for many will mistake rosy cheeks as a good sign, but this is actually just an accumulation of blood in the brain. In serious cases this will cause tinnitus, stuffiness in the head, dizziness, headaches, and bloodshot eyes. This means that the elements of water and fire in the body are totally out of balance.

"Therefore, when sitting for meditation, it is necessary to discard all external environmental factors and maintain

single-mindedness. Thinking too much will harm the kidney
qi; and when the kidney *qi* becomes weak, the lower back and
knees will easily become weak and shaky making it impossible to
continue with seated meditation. Because you have only just begun
your study of Daoism, today I'll tell you that you need to first start
by refining your physical temperament. What exactly does this
mean? It is to train one's mind to cultivate one's physical condition.
If your body is not settled, the posture will not be correct. If the
posture is not proper, the *qi* will not circulate properly and the
spirit cannot maintain oneness and peacefulness. How does one
concentrate the spirit until it becomes supple? The most important
thing is to start from having no desire. At this time you are young;
you have not had much contact with material things, fame, and
wealth, so this will be much easier for you to accomplish. I hope
that in the future you will still be able to maintain this mind of
natural innocence.

"A person's life and death are decided by the mind. The good or
evil of a human being is determined by every thought. Attention
and intention are the key ingredients in the alchemical cauldron
from which accomplishment and immortality arise. When the
mind and spirit are united and this is maintained for a period
of time, then pure *yang qi* will naturally arise; and when this
happens the alchemical cauldron heats itself. So, before you sit for
meditation, you must first empty your mind; only then can your
mind be clear. Only when the mind is clear can the spirit be steady.
This is the key to dual practice of the body and mind.

"If you do not prepare in this way, you cannot achieve. People
who do not reach the level of an immortal in this practice have
difficulty in preventing their thoughts from becoming dispersed.
Therefore, if you encounter an abundance of discursive thoughts
while in meditation or in movement practices, empty your mind
as if into the void, and slowly as the mind becomes stable, return to
your practice and incorporate your breath. Use this method often
and repeatedly, until the intention goes out in the ten directions
and the mind likewise encompasses the ten directions. In the end
you will get an experience of not arising and not dispersing, not
entering and not leaving. This is the mysterious key at the heart of
all mysteries and also the first result of practicing internal alchemy."

CHAPTER 40

THE ULTIMATE LEVEL OF DAOIST PRACTICE AND THE SEARCH FOR PERFECTION

At this point, the elder pointed at me, and this is what he said: "Earlier, you mentioned that quite often, after having meditated for a few days, you would feel an itchy sensation around the sides of the torso, or sometimes develop a rash, or experience morning erections. What happened to you at this stage is what Daoists call *yi yang lai fu*.[109] These are, to some extent, good signs. But because you are still in school, you are not in a situation where you can sit to practice when the need arises, so a remedy will be needed. You don't need to pay too much attention to these signs because if you do, you will be attached to them. Most people mistakenly regard kidneys as *kanwei*—the position of water (as per the trigrams of the *Yi Jing*). Essence can be found all over the body. Where essence is, *qi* is adjacent to it. Adding essence and *qi* together creates the authentic *kanwei*. For the time being, all you need to do is relax your body, breathe naturally, and avoid self-grasping. Apply the correct method of moving the Celestial Chariot to acquire the purest *yang qi*, so it can move freely through the eight channels. According to my experience, not all practitioners need to use the method of moving the Celestial Chariot. They can achieve the same results by practicing bringing their mind into a state of purity, void of all desire. To become proficient in this means that in any position your body may be in—whether moving or still—you need to remain mentally unperturbed. Do not cling to the senses, breathe naturally, and bring awareness to the mind at all times. In

---

109 一陽來復. The rising of *yang* energy.

this state you will have no need to pay attention to *wenhuo* and *wuhuo*.[110]

"Owing to some particular karmic connection, I was compelled to reveal everything to you today. You need to know, young man, that it's only when I was 70 years of age that I realized the true meaning of 'the essence of teachings can be written on half a sheet of paper.' Now, the corridor on the first floor, where you came in, is lined with the complete Daoist canon. But to tell you the truth, it is redundant for the wise ones, for the pith instruction can in fact be transmitted in a few words. Let me tell you, from time immemorial, there have only been two choices for those who wish to walk the path of Dao and cultivate perfection: the Path of Purity and Stillness, and the Complementary Path. Generally speaking, an ordinary practitioner needs to follow a proper sequence of transforming their essence, *qi*, and spirit, respectively, before they are able to return to the primal state of emptiness. Practitioners who practice the Path of Purity and Stillness are rare; indeed, only those with exceptional talent and wisdom will be chosen to receive the teachings. Those who walk this path are able to return to the primal state of emptiness directly (without having to go through the transforming stages).

"Our physical body is itself the microcosmos. This grotto-heaven within us is endowed with both the vessels and the capacity to perform and embody, respectively, all natural laws inherent in the macrocosmos—the changes of the four seasons, for instance. Daoists invented terms and concepts such as the eight trigrams, *yin* and *yang*, the micro- and macrocosmic orbits, and so on, to illustrate this. While there exists a supreme being in the natural world, a supreme being resides in our own body as well. This supreme being is our primary spirit, or in modern terms we could say the 'soul'—and this is also the mind. Through practices, humans can eventually return to the primal state of mind

---

110 文火, 武火. Literally, *wen* fire and *wu* fire. *Wen* fire is soft and warm, *wu* fire is hot and intense. Any exercises involving movement are considered *wu* fire, while those without movement are considered *wen* fire. Breathing that is coarse and heavy is considered *wu* fire, while breathing that is light and fine is considered *wen* fire. Using mental energy is considered *wu* fire, and using intention is considered *wen* fire.

that is pure, and free of suffering, worries, and troubles. When the primal state is restored, neither exerting oneself, nor pushing and experimenting with *qi* and breath are necessary. When ceasing to pursue, the mind becomes utterly unfettered, and the body is in optimal condition. At this point, go a step further and gather a mind free of delusive thoughts, uniting *qi* and spirit—a state that, in Daoist terms, can be referred to as completing one's true spiritual self. The unification of spirit and *qi* is indeed achievable and the the practitioner can separate their spirit and body freely, thereby manifesting themselves into indefinite forms."

CHAPTER 41

REITERATING THE IMPORTANCE OF THE BREATH AND THE TONGUE

Owing to his 50 years of experience in guiding numerous people, the elder reiterated the following: "While in stillness, allow your eyes to be half open and half closed, first finding the tip of your nose, then extending your gaze relaxedly toward a point in front of you. Doing this will help focus your spirit and mind and prevent any dissipation of awareness. When your breath is fast, remember you only need to lightly press the tip of your tongue on the line where the top teeth and the gums converge; however, if your breath is soft and weak like strands of silk, you will then need to regulate it by curling up your tongue while inhaling and curling it downward while exhaling."

Daoists pay great attention to the marvelous effects of the tongue—the term "rousing the red dragon" refers to its various movements and its connection to the vital organs of our body, in addition to its role as the bridge to get through to the channels. In Traditional Chinese Medicine, diagnosis through observation of a patient's appearance is not restricted to viewing their complexion. By examining the upper side of the tongue one can see the state and functioning of the heart, liver, spleen, and stomach. For instance, when there is blazing heat in the heart, the tip of the tongue will appear notably crimson. On the other hand, a healthy person with a balanced diet—whose stomach *qi* is thus in harmony—will have a tongue of just the right color, fairly moist, and with a normal coating that is not too thick. The root of the tongue is the area representing the kidneys, whereas its sides are observed to gain insight into the patient's liver and gallbladder. The state of one's vital organs and blood, as well as the amount of body fluids, is closely connected to the tongue. For example, if when a person sticks their tongue out you can clearly see cracks similar to those on a turtle's shell, then it is usually an indication that their *qi* and blood are both deficient, while the heat is in surplus, causing the individual to be in poor health. Observing the patient's pulse in addition to their tongue can then help the physician to determine how to nourish *yin* energy and increase *qi*, expel dampness, strengthen the spleen, and so on. All things considered, the tongue is a compendium of information on the health of the body.

The reason why Daoist practitioners swirl the tongue inside the mouth during their meditation practice is that the excess saliva thus created is swallowed down to the *dantian*, thereby harmonizing the energy of the vital organs to avoid chronic diseases from developing. This is also very effective in calming the nerves and reducing heat in the body. Often when the long-term residents of the temple do their morning *qi* bathing exercises and get to the step that involves the root of the tongue, I tell the practitioners to first completely relax their facial muscles by smiling in front of a mirror or just holding a grin. This is followed by opening the mouth widely several times and then by sticking the tongue out and retracting it 36 times to stretch its muscles and nerves. The tongue is then circled around the upper palate and then around the underside of the mouth while swishing the excess saliva, much as you would do after brushing your teeth. When this is done, regulate the breath and calm the mind before dividing a mouthful of saliva into three equal parts and swallowing to the *dantian* successively. Over many years, I have heard people who practice this say that they no longer need sleeping pills. Those who suffered from problems with their facial nerves and practiced this exercise, along with some topical massage, made speedy recoveries. It follows that we must never take the tongue for granted!

If you notice that your mind begins to drift after sitting for a while, you may gently close the eyes and bring your awareness to the *dantian*. Breathe—exhaling the old and inhaling the new— and when your mind and spirit are unified again, open your eyes halfway and continue to practice. If you feel heavy, drowsy, and unable to focus on any acupoint, clench your hands into fists with the thumbs pressed against the root of the ring fingers, then place the fists facing downward on your inner thighs near the groin and stretch the arms, staring straight ahead with eyes wide open. Repeat this a few times until any remaining drowsiness is cleared. If the mind is filled with frivolous, negative, or obsessive thoughts or wild fantasies, then simply observe these thoughts a while. You can also visualize them exiting with each exhalation and congealing into a spot about a fist's distance in front of the tip of the nose. Continue doing so until the mind is calm again, then resume your meditation.

CHAPTER 42

WHEN THE SENSES ARE COLLECTED, ANGER CANNOT ARISE

"The most vital components of our lives are essence and spirit. These are also the main sources of energy in our body. Generally speaking, the key to cultivating one's inner alchemy lies in essence and spirit. Specifically, lead is a metaphor for one's essence and *qi*, whereas mercury is symbolic of spirit. It's imperative, therefore, to cultivate one's essence, *qi*, and spirit from a young age to avoid a run-down in health as well as deficiency in lead and mercury in middle age. When a person's spirit is adequate, their *qi* will be abundant. When the spirit is lucid, essence will naturally thrive. The lucidity of one's essence, *qi*, and spirit are the most important fundamental elements in Daoism." This was the enlightening instruction that the elder continued to give us.

Next, he turned to me and imparted the following: "In general, men aged between 13 and 25 are at their peak of *yang qi*. When their *yang qi* even slightly arises, they simply cannot control their desires, which results in excessive detrimental leakage [of sperm]. This is the biggest harm one can do to one's body in relation to essence, *qi*, and spirit. So you really must pay attention to this. This is the predicament that in the past made scores of Daoist practitioners stumble. Consequently, the proper handling of excessive *yang qi* is instrumental in making or breaking a practitioner's spiritual attainment in the later stage. It should not be taken lightly. Most young men do not understand the significance of this: letting their vital essence go to waste. You must know that every drop of water will eventually form a river."

At this point, a fellow practitioner seized on a short pause in the elder's exposition and asked the following question: "Presently we are trying our best with the help of instruction. At times we activate the micro- and macrocosmic orbits. We know, however, that being able to do that is still miles away from attaining the great Dao. So we would like to ask the master to point out to us a path to attainment involving practice of the mind, rather than just using the physical body, so that if the physical methods do not work we still have a gleam of hope."

Having heard this sincere request, the old master nodded and continued his discourse: "The fact that you asked this question shows that you have been diligent in your practice for you've touched on the subject of the ultimate enlightenment. The path to enlightenment is an arduous task for most. A handful of individuals have managed to be still most of the time, to not be attached to what they see and hear, and to avoid disputes and gossip. This kind of mind is akin to that of a hibernating animal. Yet nothing is more critical than making sure the mind is utterly unfettered and the physical body in optimal condition. Daoist terminologies such as *Xuanguan* and *Qiaowei* are employed as an alternative to help those with lower-intermediate levels of capacity to understand. The foundation of Dao can only be achieved through *hundun*.[111] The idea of *hundun* here refers to the state where a practitioner becomes one with the universe, sharing the same root with heaven and earth. Only by focusing on unifying the essence, *qi*, and spirit, can one experience and achieve the state of *hundun*, and only then does the practitioner have the opportunity to attain the primal unadulterated state and absorb the energy of the universe.

"An experienced teacher will then inform the practitioner that such experience serves as the best time to see one's true nature and collect medicine to obtain the purest *yang qi*. A sharp practitioner will always be ready to grab any opportunity to practice, whenever or wherever it presents itself. When still, sit in meditation; when in movement, practice the mind. According to my own personal experience, true meditation takes place in the midst of the most

---

111 混沌. Literally, "primal chaos" (the original formless state of the universe before creation).

clamorous situations, when the meditator maintains calm without giving rise to anger. In a noisy marketplace, they are like a pure and serene maiden. The merits of achieving this are superior to 1,000 meditation sessions. The great Dao is uncomplicated wondrous emptiness. In your leisure time, regulate your breath and collect your spirit and *qi* in the area just below your navel. Count your breaths as they come in and out until they number into the thousands. If you are able to remain calm during the counting, then collect the six gates. You will slowly come to the point where you feel the whole world around you, and it seems that the whole world around you, including your breath, comes to a stop. In this state, it's like the way a cat keeps a watchful eye on the mouse. No need to forcefully pursue—just knowing is enough. Gradually, a surge of *yang qi* will naturally emerge of itself.

"I might need to elaborate a little on the concept of 'collecting the six gates' for you youngsters. They refer to the urethra, mouth, eyes, ears, nose, and the mind. An ancient Daoist immortal once said: 'If the upper gates are open, fire cannot be ignited; without the fire, inner alchemy won't be completed. If the lower gates are open, fire cannot be ignited; without the fire, how will the "golden pill" be attained?' All past sages held single-minded focus as the key to obtaining the golden pill. While I mention this, I have a personal tip for you: If in the future you have the chance to practice the movement of the Celestial Chariot—the method to open all the channels in the body—you ought to visualize storing your *qi* in your *dantian* during inhalation. Make sure you place the tip of your tongue upon the upper palate. The saliva produced in this manner is the nectar of immortality with marvelous qualities and will neutralize all delusive thoughts in the mind. Make sure your teeth are tightly closed and place your awareness on the in- and out-breath so the mind is merged with the breath." This was the advice offered to us three young beginners by the senior practitioner.

He then continued: "At times, when one enters deeper meditative stillness, one might experience a sudden surge of brightness that illuminates the mind. It is akin to the borderless sky that encompasses all happenings, yet remains unmoved. When joyous things arise, don't feel complacent. Likewise, your mind should not yield to the upheaval brought about by calamities. It is also comparable to how despite changing clothes each day, the body of flesh and bones stays the same. When some practitioners achieve this state, they think it is the achievement of practice through body and mind, while they ought to hold to a mind that does not move whilst according itself to circumstances. If a practitioner harbors delight in his heart, he might incur the loss of hard-earned accomplishments due to his tendency to fret over gain and loss."

Right about then, the elder's attendant knocked on the door to inform him that two disciples were waiting in the parlor, and asked what the master would have him do. The elder raised his head and waved his hand to indicate that he knew. The three of us looked at each other, wondering whether we had taken up too much of the master's time. Picking up on our noticeable concern, the senior uttered: "Nothing to worry about! Let me make my last point. The key to meditation is to be at peace wherever you go and maintain a tranquil mind at all times. The breath should consistently be smooth and even, with your awareness on both the inhalation and exhalation allowing you to regularly enter a state of extreme stillness. This kind of utmost mental quiescence is in actual fact the primary spirit and the original *qi* (referring to the mind) according to Daoist terminology. However, all Daoist schools of thought simply refer to this as having 'opened the gate of the taiji' (the ultimate or absolute). The so-called 'true seed' is the original *qi* stemming from the void. If a practitioner is able to grasp the opportunity while they get hold of the 'true seed' to turn the Celestial Chariot, what they could achieve is indeed invaluable. This is the ultimate attainment of all practitioners. However, those with limited experience are simply at a loss when this type of *qi* arises in their meditative stillness. This is an important point to pay attention to.

"A lot of practitioners quite enjoy the state of 'emptiness' through their meditation practice. This in fact requires great caution. No matter how placid your meditation allows you to become, retain a watchful awareness within your original spirit; otherwise you will not reach a high state. In the end, one will reside continuously in the truth with the brightness of alert and knowing awareness. This is where the 'true medicine' dwells and is also the true way to 'create the golden pill.' No matter how high your meditative state seems to be, this is the method to preserve it, like a dragon guarding its pearls. The Daoist immortal Chu Yuyang once instructed: 'The one thing that exists within emptiness is true *yin*; while the ability to preserve one's essence in the midst of ultimate emptiness is true *yang*.' Deploying this method will enable the practitioner to obtain the ultimate medicine of spiritual achievement."

CHAPTER 43

A DELIGHTFUL CONNECTION WITH DIVINITY AND DAOISM

The respectable elder had been practicing Daoism for decades, and he was getting ready to divulge all of his knowledge to me. He started by saying: "The true essence must wait for oral instruction; otherwise how can one further increase the energy of the body? The greatest taboo for one wishing to take part in authentic spiritual practice, that which blocks the way to the blossoming of their understanding, is to adopt a narrow and partial view on things. It is prohibited for someone who wants to learn and practice the Dao to confound his own chance at enlightenment by drawing conclusions from limited information. A frog in a well could never fathom such a thing as a dragon's cave. A raven could never fathom the concept of a phoenix living on earth. It's no coincidence that we have the affinity to meet today. It is because of our karmic connection. I place a very high value on the karmic connections between people. The value of this can be seen in the way that Zhang Liang[112] followed Chi Songtzi[113] to learn, and also when the Yellow Emperor[114] sought teachings from Guang Chentzi[115] on Kongtong Mountain.[116] All occurred just as destiny dictated. I will definitely not withhold anything from you because of your youth. The Great Path belongs to everybody, and anyone with a connection with

---

112 張良. Fugitive-turned-strategist and an advisor to generals and leaders during the establishment of the Han dynasty.

113 赤松子. A highly achieved immortal who lived during the Qing and Han Dynasty.

114 黃帝. A leader who lived over 5,000 years ago in China. He is said to be the forefather of the Chinese race.

115 廣成子. Said to be the incarnation of one of the members of the Trinity, the three highest Gods in Daoism.

116 崆峒山. Mountains sacred to the Daoist tradition, located in the city of Pingliang, Gansu province, China.

it will understand it. After tomorrow, you and I will never meet again. Therefore, I will tell you everything I know, in the hope that you will be able to share it, and in future times refine and develop it."

My own connection with the Path of Immortals is something of a happy accident. I was my aunt's favorite nephew, and she introduced me to *Yi Guan Dao* when I was 17. There, I received much undeserved kindness from the elders. I met an elder from the the mainland who was in his early 70s. He knew that I liked sitting meditation, and so he often shared techniques and parables about it. He once told me that he had had interactions with Chen Yingning in Shanghai, and that they were both friends and teachers to each other. Chen Yingning was a lay practitioner who took refuge in the Dragon's Gate Sect of the Daoist School of Complete Reality. He had delved deeply into the Path of the Immortals. At that time, because Chen had a monthly magazine and often held speeches, this elder frequently discussed with him contents of the book *San Tong Qi*,[117] and he also became acquainted with some of Chen's disciples. After coming to Taiwan, by coincidence he met a disciple of Chen, whose last name was Yuan. The elder told me that this Daoist master, Chen Yingning, had made a very great contribution to the Path of Immortals and Daoism in modern times. He often visited places where Chen held speeches and answered Chen's invitations. At that time, Chen had about 100 students, the majority being women, but most of them left after a period of time. Chen was not discouraged by this. He combined medicine and science and matched them up with the principles found in the *Yi Jing*. In this way, he naturally began to attract a number of students who liked Daoism and began to follow him and practice under his guidance.

According to this elder, the people whom he had interactions with after he came to Taiwan included: the Daoist master Liu Peizhong of the Kunlun Immortal Sect; the Daoist master Zhen Shizi, who lived in Keelung; and Doctor Sun, who at that time lived in Hong Kong. At that time there were special events being held in

---

117 參同契.

the Buddhist hall. This elder joined and invited me to eat with him and we also spoke at tea times between meals. He frequently spoke of his knowledge and concepts about sitting meditation. This was of great help to me during my studies.

He often talked about Master Zhu Zhuzi (Zhu Xi), and said that in fact, sitting meditation and Daoist practice could be integrated. He said that the "non-indulgence" advocated by Master Zhu Zhuzi was not just an act of the body, but also required collecting the mind and spirit. Zhu Zhuzi suggested that scholars concentrate their mind on their studies, whether in stillness, in motion, or while dreaming, and focus on the meaning to be found between the lines. A person won't be able to study well if they cannot find single-minded focus. If one could truly understand Master Zhu's theory of "investigating truth and non-indulgence," it would be a great help to nourishing one's *qi* and spiritual energy. Zhu Zhuzi also advocated the Confucian sitting meditation method, as evidenced in many of his teaching materials. More than once, he told his students that sitting meditation was mandatory for collecting the body and mind. He also said once that if the mind starts to spread outward in search of material goods or forms and sounds, meditation is necessary to quickly redirect it. Even more importantly, Zhu Zhuzi mentioned that the purpose of sitting meditation is not to reach for immortality or realize the truth. It was rather, to provide a resting place for the mind when the student becomes exhausted during the rigors of his learning, without letting it wander astray amidst hardships.

The elder spoke to me many a time about the contents of the *San Tong Qi*, quoting from other classics on two occasions, and allowing me a taste of the beauty of the work. The book was permeated with the rationale of Daoism as well as the *Yi Jing* in both primordial and manifested arrangements, establishing a robust foundation in me during the period of time. This period enabled me to grow the stablest of roots. It would not be an overstatement to say that Wei Boyang's *San Tong Qi* is a vitally important book for both the present and the future. Its significance is unparalleled by almost all Daoist literature since.

CHAPTER 44

NOTES ON MEDITATION FOR BOTH MEN AND WOMEN

I once asked the elder, Master He, a few questions related to essence, *qi*, and spirit. He replied rather frankly: "Men often face a somewhat embarrassing situation; that is, nocturnal emissions and ejaculation. Lacking a method to restore their vital essence will undoubtedly lead to such a predicament as they grow up. It is primarily caused by the deficiency and depletion of kidney water and *qi*.[118] According to Chinese medical theory, this condition can be remedied by, according to the patient's constitution, taking medicinal herbs and substances such as cistanche, Chinese dodder seeds, oyster, or deer velvet. This, however, does not treat the root of the problem." Due to his prior experience as a Chinese Medicine practitioner, Master He taught me a method to remedy the problem. It involves grinding down certain herbs into a powder and placing them on the navel, taped down with a gauze dressing and plasters. He also taught me the following method he learned from Daoist Master Zhen Shizi.

Hold a big imaginary ball in front of your chest. Press it against the chest whilst inhaling and contracting the anus. While doing this, raise your tailbone to allow the *qi*'s ascension to the top of your head. As the *qi* is ascending, lift the shoulders to the ears and hold till you breathe to the fullest. Exhale, relaxing the shoulders and anus. Repeat this movement sequence 7–21 times. Master He has taught these movements and sequences to a lot of people, with good results. It is nonetheless preferable, for safety reasons, that an experienced master demonstrate it in person. For young

---

118 腎水和腎氣不足 (*shenshuiheshenqibuzu*). The kidneys relate to the water element, according to the five elements theory. When the kidney water and *qi* become depleted, back pain as well as sexual dysfunction, such as listed above, can occur.

male practitioners, it is recommended that they don't focus their awareness on the lower *dantian* area for too long. If they must, they should not overexert themselves during the practice. Female practitioners are advised to avoid focusing their awareness on the same area a week before their period is due to start and during menstruation.

He once mentioned to me that because high blood pressure runs in the family, his systolic pressure would soar to 200 even if he just slightly overworked or kept an irregular schedule. At one point, due to excessive overwork, a stroke left his right eye completely blind. Owing to his karmic connection with the Daoist master Zhen Shizi, he received some tips from the master himself on meditation. The master instructed him to sit eight times a day, each session to last for at least a half-hour. He did just that, as well as taking medication prescribed by the doctor. Two weeks later, he could feel the facial nerves start to relax, the swelling in his eye reduced, and congestion started to ease up. A month later, he experienced a surge of warm *qi* from his legs up to the *dantian* area. Eventually, even his hands benefited from the practice and became warm. Another month went by, after which he stopped his medicine while his blood pressure went down to normal as did his blood sugar levels. At that point, he would often feel a surge of warm *qi* scuttling and moving up and down in the lower abdomen, resulting in an indescribable sense of comfort. He knew for himself that not only had he recovered from his illness, he had become healthier.

Master He also gave me a thorough account of the oral tips on techniques for the joining of water and fire and heaven and earth[119] that he received from Master Si. It was a comprehensive account of practices on both the micro- and macrocosmic orbits as well how to achieve the inner pill, both drawing from Master Si's conscientious studies of the *Dan Jing* and his profound understanding of the *Yi Jing*. Master Si was able to apply the cryptic interpretation of descriptions accompanying the hexagrams from the *Yi Jing* to his

---

119 坎離, 乾坤交配的技巧 (*kanli, qiankunjiaopeidejiqiao*). These are referring to the trigrams of water (*kun*) and fire (*li*), as well as heaven (*qian*) and earth (*kun*) from the *Book of Changes* (*Yi Jing*).

own spiritual practices. He had already affected the sublimation of his being through spiritual cultivation. One can say his level of spiritual attainment is that of perfection. Master He once told me: "In the future when you are applying yourself to the foundational practices for Daoist cultivation building the foundation, remember that the important thing is to do it without excessive force. When the foundations of your practice have truly been established and no frivolous thoughts arise, you can without the least exertion give rise to it again. Bear in mind that unless you put to rest all worldly worries and cares then true rest will never be obtained, not even to mention gathering the medicine."

CHAPTER 45

USING ARM SWINGING EXERCISE TO ASSIST MEDITATION

Master He also mentioned how lucky he was to have met Master Luo Chunppu, known as "the Immortal Luo." In Minshan, Master Luo had a huge following and many disciples. Master He received from him transmissions of scores of pith instructions, including the one on sleeping *qigong* passed on directly from Master Chen Tuan, the legendary Daoist sage. Master He also instructed me on the practice of "Arm Swinging."

He gave the following instructions: "Before swinging your arms, stand with feet shoulder-width apart. Wear no socks or shoes, and preferably be on the grass so your feet can absorb the essence from the earth. Begin visualizing, from the top of your head all the way down to the soles of your feet, that your body is slowly loosening up like a deflating balloon. Repeat this three times. Next, regulate your breath by inhaling slowly until the *qi* settles into the *dantian*, then exhale through the nose, three times. Now, bring awareness to the lower abdomen and completely relax this area. Avoid holding your breath; just gently keep your awareness in the lower abdomen about 4 fingers' width below the belly button while performing the arm swinging. Keep your arms straight and your palms flat. The muscles and even the skeletal structure must be completely relaxed, without exerting unnecessary force.

"In the beginning stage, just make sure your mind, muscles, and joints are all summarized by a single word: 'relaxed.' Swing your arms back with about 70 percent of your force, and allow them to bounce back with about 30 percent of your force. Gently grasp the earth with your toes when the arms swing backward— this will enhance blood and *qi* circulation and stimulate bowel movement. You should notice some perspiration and warmth in your stomach—signs of good blood and *qi* circulation. Your eyes should look straight ahead to a distant point, with a relaxed gaze. Try to use your intention instead of force while doing this. When the aforementioned symptoms arise, you may close your eyes, yet still maintain your gaze toward a distant point in front of you. Doing this can help collect the spirit, *qi*, and essence in one place. This is particularly beneficial for replenishing one's spirit and *qi*. Past sages were able to unblock their *qi* and blood. Coupling this with meditation, they eventually unlocked both micro- and macrocosmic orbits.

"If the goal is to open the eight extraordinary channels, place awareness on the *tanzhong* acupoint—located in the middle of the chest—while swinging the arms and breathing. Breathe in and out through the nostrils. You can supplement this with movement practices when your mind is more able to focus. This is because when the mind is filled with delusive thoughts and worries, your *qi* and blood are prone to blockage; or, if the mind is scattered or lacks focus, your *qi* will gradually condense and solidify, forming a wall within. Therefore, while swinging the arms, you should not be distracted by external stimuli. Some of the ailments caused by an overactive, scattered mind include ringing in the ears, discomfort in the teeth, or skin rashes, all of which account for the symptoms of vacuous heat rising in the body.[120] When these symptoms are present, you should take a short break from the exercise and regulate your breath. Breathe naturally, keep your gaze and hearing inward, and refrain from actively listening and speaking. In a relaxed manner, bring your awareness back to your breath. You may do this in either seated or standing position—the point is to bring all of your scattered thoughts to a halt. When you regain the focus, you may resume the 'Arm Swinging' exercise.

"When your practice of this method deepens, the benefits will increase as well. These include stronger *yuan qi*,[121] kidneys, liver, lungs, stomach, and spleen. If you wish to take your practice even further, you can couple it with some breathing techniques to

---

120 虛火上身 (*xu huo shang shen*). In Chinese Medicine, this is a condition in which heat rises in the body due to vacuity (also translated as "deficiency").
121 元氣. Can be translated as "original *qi*." It is the foundation of *qi* in the body.

allow the *qi* to fill the entire body. At this point, you need to ensure that your *qi* is still and not outflowing—maintain the *qi* within the body, and the mind as calm and collected as a waveless pond. Gradually learn to control your breathing, leading it from shallow to deep, to the point where you can feel the *qi* coming out of your skin. Eventually, you will go a step further and the *qi* will slowly move on to permeate the bones and massage the internal organs. You may take breaks between rounds, during which you can do the following routine to help eliminate toxins: Take a deep breath and divide it into three small exhalations. Repeat this seven times. Do this in a relaxed manner; never exert to the point of dizziness, headaches, and nausea."

Over a period of time, Master He transmitted a supplementary practice to meditation that involves bringing awareness to various acupoints. He also said: "While swinging the arms, you may bring focus between the eyebrows, but those with high blood pressure or people with blood and *qi* issues should not keep their attention placed on that point." He also explained very clearly how to unblock all the *qi* that may be stagnant in the body. Apparently, Master He had perfected this skill while living in Sichuan province. Indeed, if he had not told me his age, my first impression was of a man in his early 50s. The whiteness of his complexion always bore a certain rosy luster. Also, he was well mannered; he was alert and agile whether still or moving, in a way equal to any young man. At that time he was diligent in the joint practice of meditation and arm swinging. During those ten years, he did not catch a single cold and only extremely rarely did any headaches bother him. He once instructed me concerning guarding the acupoints. He mentioned that, at the earlier stages of practice, it is not suitable to guard any particular point too intently. It suffices to put one's earnest effort into breathing naturally on every inhalation and exhalation.

CHAPTER **46**

MEDITATION AND *QIGONG* TECHNIQUES FOR WHEN THE *YANG QI* IS STRONG

There are no lack of books on the subject of Daoist practice. Under no circumstances should you rely on a book to support your practice. A great number of people have been misled by the frequently confused presentation of *yin-yang*, the eight trigrams, as well as water and fire, from the *Yi Jing* trigrams. The life of the practice can only be passed from teacher to student through a lineage; the spirit can then be personally experienced.

I was advised to meditate when the *yang qi* is flourishing, between the hours of 11pm and 1am. If I were to meditate at this time, the effects would be better. What Zhuangzi really meant when he said "The true man breathes from the heels" was that one's breath can gradually, through meditation and breath regulation, "sink" deeper and deeper until one becomes so immersed that one naturally reaches the state of silent stillness. It is not that one breath is taken and drawn straight down to the soles of the feet. When you have a chance, look to how newborn babies breathe: They make fists with both hands and place them on the belly as it rises and falls. This is a great secret. When the breathing moves to a deeper level it will become more like that of a turtle. Finally, you will attain turtle breathing, which means that you have practiced to the point where your acquired breathing pattern has transformed back into your original prenatal breathing pattern. According to Daoism, the three *dantians* of the body are the upper *dantian* at the top of the head, the middle *dantian* in the center of the chest, and the lower *dantian* just below the navel.

Teacher He mentioned that, without fail, every time he urinates, he will be very careful to remember what he was taught about lifting the heels of the feet, locking the anus, and segmenting the stream of urine; clenching the teeth and looking up, balling the fists and focusing all attention on the area between the kidneys. He said that practicing in this way will help the vital energy. The adrenal glands above the kidneys must not be overlooked. These are the source of all life and where the source of the *yang qi* cultivated in meditation resides. Teacher He would quote a phrase spoken to him by Master Luo: "Take the Daoist pill of immortality to unify the mind and spirit, attaining a state beyond mortal capacity, restore your original essence to replenish the brain and attain limitless life with no worries." Slowly he came to experience this.

Teacher He long held the practice of *cunxiang*[122] in high regard. This practice entails keeping the mind free of distracting thoughts and remaining absorbed on the one breath. He once took the time to explain what marvel is concealed in this "one"; the meaning of "one," in the term "one breath." For him, it was quite a marvelous concept; indeed, it refers to an absence of all coming and going. In this state, the thoughts have neither come nor departed, and the breath neither enters nor exits; neither the thoughts nor the breath have an identifiable coming or going. What kind of state is this? It is similar to a statement of Laozi: "Amid chaos there is phenomena, amid chaos there are objects."

The *Yellow Court Classic* also pointed to this several times. So this focusing on the "one breath" is in other words single-pointed awareness. When the mind is collected into the spirit, the true *qi* will naturally emerge, and the true *yang* will be replete of itself.

I once asked Master He how we might practice breath control with "single-pointed awareness" and swallow the breath. His response was basically: "In the beginning, do not impose any restriction on the breath: Just let it come in and out smoothly, unhindered, free of any stagnation. When you reach a stage where the body is at ease and the mind peaceful, regulate the inhalations and exhalations through the nose. At first you can practice in this

---

122 存想. A practice of gathering and utilizing the spirit and essence.

way: On the inhalation, direct the breath to the *dantian*. Then, while holding the breath, count silently. When you are unable to hold any longer, exhale slowly through the mouth. Repeat the process, increasing the time you hold the breath at the *dantian*. Fetal breathing will naturally arise after a time. When I just began, I did not restrict myself but allowed my breath to come in smoothly, without stopping. When I got to the point that the body and mind became settled, I began to breathe through my nose and practiced breathing directly to the *dantian*. Then I closed my mouth, and counted silently to myself until I was unable to hold the breath any longer. Then I breathed out through the mouth and like this, the term of breath retention could slowly be increased. Then I began to use the nose to take small breaths down to the *dantian* and as I was able to hold the breath longer, the practice would slowly improve.

"Focus the mind at a point 4½ fingers' distance below the belly button, in concentrated attention. Breathe naturally at first, and finally breathe into this point below the navel. This is called 'regulating the breath.' When mind and breath become intertwined, they will follow each other. In the end, the mind and body will become tranquil. In this state, the practice is neither contrived nor too lax. This is the stage of not losing the practice and not forcing it. The mind is not to be found externally. When the mind is calm, it will slowly enter into a state of stillness. This is called 'dropping the mind,' but this is not like the total absence of light. A turtle in a dark cave can still see. You need to focus on the *dantian*, and maintain this regardless of whether you're reclining, sitting, standing, or moving, in all places and at all times.

"The most important thing is that that when you are in meditation you focus your mind and all your concentration on the *dantian*. After a time the *qi* will accumulate around the large intestines and the breath will join with the *dantian*. Slowly *qi* will fill the eight greater channels as well as the lesser channels of the body. Every day, at all times, focus on this area below the belly button. Imagine there is a warm current flowing out of the *dantian*. Regardless of whether this is in stillness or movement, imagine this current. After a period of time, the belly button will develop a sensation of heat that will be present at all times. This heat will burn up all diseases.

When sitting in meditation, collect the saliva in the mouth. This will be effective every time you swallow. The more saliva that you swallow, the more the vital organs will be regulated. When the fire in the heart is reduced and the water rises in the kidneys, this is called 'the water and fire elements combining for their mutual benefit.'[123] At this time the internal alchemy can become complete.

"The *yang qi* is at its peak when the sun is out, and especially during the hours just before and after dawn, between 3am to 7am, when it has just begun to rise. This is when the *yang qi* has just come up. You can face east or south at this time, sit in full lotus to meditate, and allow clean *qi* to enter and leave the body with the breath. While doing this, saliva will naturally fill the mouth. When the mouth is full, swallow while lightly contracting the muscle of the anus. Practice this repeatedly. If you begin to lose your breath, then drop the head down, open the mouth a little bit, and slowly exhale."

It seemed as if Master He had a strong karmic connection to me. By increments, he slowly shared with me all of the tips he picked up throughout his period of study in Sichuan, leaving nothing out. Master He mentioned that he met with an old practitioner during his time on Chengdu mountain who had used this method to practice for a long time. This old practitioner had transformed his white hair into the thick black hair of a young man. All of his original teeth fell out and new teeth came in to replace them. All year round, regardless of the season or weather, he always wore the same set of simple monk's robes. He lived on into his 15th decade before disappearing. Nobody was able to track him down after that and his name is known in legend now.

Master He had once mentioned how books on lovemaking were very popular among the book stalls on the street. He said that since the time of the Han dynasty this was in vogue. However, he said that this was regarded as an external path and under no circumstances should we fall into it. There are more than ten schools that know about this. Some said it could cure diseases like consumption or gather *yin* and nourish *yang* energy. Actually,

---

123 水火既濟 (*shuihuojiji*).

most people participate only in order to satisfy their own personal desires. However, one must be careful with these practices. If you were to practice these, at best one would only "restore the essence to nourish the brain." Actually, the valuable area associated with meditation is within the periphery of the belly button. The lower burner referred to by ancient people here is below the belly button. The area above the belly button is referred to as the cauldron. For the practitioners who have obtained oral instructions, you go through your own body, the lower and middle burners, to practice. Mainly, we want to transform desire for the purpose of increasing life energy.

Master He worked hard to explain everything as clearly as he possibly could. In the end he advised me to read Lu Chunyang's *Bai Zi Ming*,[124] and Zhang Ziyang's *Pure Enlightenment Scrawl*.[125]

He would always advise me to read the writings of the ancient immortals. Once you practice diligently and experience it for yourself, you must heed the words and experiences more experienced practitioners have spoken to us and meld these into your practice. In this way, you will slowly but surely improve. When this is accompanied with diligence and experience, slowly there will be improvement.

This is the story of an auspicious connection I held with the elder He on the Path of Immortals. This wise and saintly man has now left our world, and his bearing still appears clearly in my mind. I can only express gratitude to him again and again.

---

124 百字銘.
125 悟真篇 (*Wu Zhen Pian*).

CHAPTER 47

ADJUSTING THE BREATH
TO PROTECT THE BODY

No Need to Mention Strange Powers or Gods

In the winter of 1979, my Daoist master from the School of Complete Reality went on a trip with two attendants. They were driving on a particularly steep and bumpy area of Yangde Road in the Yangming Mountains of Taipei. They happened to be following a delivery truck that unexpectedly stopped. The attendant who was driving the car, not having enough time to react, slammed into the rear end of the truck. In the collision, the windshield was shattered, but oddly enough neither my teacher nor his two attendants sustained any injury. The driver of the truck was visibly shaken and he anxiously rushed over to apologize. The other attendant, who hadn't been driving, got out of the car and met him to resolve the matter. This whole process took about two hours and in the interim the master sat without the slightest movement, with eyes closed, adjusting his breath. The attendant returned to the car and prepared to depart, but the engine wouldn't start. He continued in his attempts to start the engine for about ten minutes, but it wasn't until the teacher opened both of his eyes and took a breath that the engine could be started. I later heard this story from the two attendants.

The master said: "In the instant when the collision occurred, I very naturally slid into embryonic breathing, and used my true *qi* to suppress my original spirit to ensure that my spirit would not leave my body. Perhaps it was this action that had an impact on the car. Later I noticed that the car wouldn't start, so once more I adjusted my breath." My brother disciples shared this short episode in secret. With regard to the details of the matter, the disciples were told by the master not to indiscriminately share stories of spiritual matters. It was only after our master reached the age of 70 that facts, such as this car accident, came out. It was also revealed that after having sustained an injury to his bladder at this time, our master undertook a year of self-treatment, with the help of medicinal plants, meditation, and breathing practice. By using these alone, he gradually made a full recovery.

One Sunday I visited the master. On this occasion he motioned to me to come over to the tea table by his small couch to sit. He then proceeded to question me: "Half a year ago I mentioned to you some of the golden pill practice methods from the *Pure Enlightenment Scrawl.* Is there anything about this writing that you do not understand?" The master was concerned that I could not understand it, so he made a special effort to make a very clear explanation. In particular, he made mention of the use of certain medicinal herbs, the micro- and macrocosmic orbits. Every sect had different explanations. There are also differences between the concepts of pre- and post-heaven.[126] So, my master once again reminded me: "When doing raising and lowering, as well as revolving movements, you absolutely must pay attention that the strength of the breath must match the concentration even more than on normal days. Only then will there be a distinct result." The master said that at this time, the most important thing was to rely on the explanation and reminders of an experienced master. Otherwise, nine times out of ten, you'll end up spending a lot of time making mistakes. Actually, my master has had a lot of unique experiences. He probably understood my situation at that time from the condition of my body and mind. Because he noticed that even though it was winter and quite windy I was still wearing only a short-sleeved shirt, he asked me if I had recently experienced tinnitus. He also asked me if my waist often felt very hot and if this was followed by my whole body feeling feverish.

I answered : "I certainly have been experiencing this. Also, in the past, after sitting in meditation for 15–30 minutes, I would have a sensation of heat in my abdomen, coming from my kidneys. But

---

126 先天後天 (*xiantianhoutian*). Pre-heaven and post-heaven are different arrangements of the trigrams in the *Book of Changes* (*Yi Jing*).

recently, in the past two months, when I sit for meditation, before ten minutes have passed, I get the sensation of intense heat as if my body has been wrapped in a great number of quilts." The master nodded his head, meaning that he could understand my condition. After this, he gave me an explanation of how I could practice the microcosmic orbit more often, and then told me to practice and see.

CHAPTER 48

NON-ATTACHMENT TO STATES

When Demons Come, Strike Them Down

In reality, this condition of mine had been ongoing. Whether walking or sleeping, I could feel a warm sensation that would follow my *qi* from the lower abdomen to the kidneys, where it would heat up like a fire. In the past my master had said that when the channel was about to open, it would be preempted by certain signs. At this time, one must know how to coordinate the circulation with the breath. In addition, coordinating the body with the mental states becomes even more important. Sometimes, it would feel as though insects were constantly crawling back and forth along certain parts of my body. Following this, depending on where the *qi* passed, various experiences might come up, and there would be a great many possibilities for what the practitioner might experience. The guidance of an experienced practitioner was certainly needed. This became undeniably clear to me through my own experiences. I am truly thankful for my master's graciousness!

I continued to practice meditation regularly according to my master's instructions, incorporating breath and *qi* circulation. Several times while I was in the middle of this practice, I experienced the breath becoming still. My master's advice in this case was: "Let it be and continue to practice. Don't be disturbed by anything."

There were also many occasions while practicing the microcosmic orbit, when I entered into stillness. Sometimes I would see a light and a shadow when the *qi* moved from the back of my head toward my forehead, stopping for a time at the *yintang* acupoint, the space between the eyebrows. I had also asked my master about these experiences, and he would repeat that same advice: "Disregard this experience and continue to practice. Don't give attention to any particular state. When you meet the Buddha in meditation, kill the Buddha; when you meet a demon, kill the demon."

When I think back now on these experiences, I feel that without a master's guidance, so many people would waste time practicing blindly. Some people like to look at the lights, and some mentally unstable people would think that they saw a bodhisattva. They see images and become very pleased with themselves and become attached to this state. Of course, this whole process happened over the course of one year, and there were several other states and experiences and changes that occurred to my body. These were states I had to disregard.

From a medical perspective, these also have their explanations. Because the paths of the micro- and macrocosmic orbits pass by many different parts of the sympathetic nervous system, all of the important glands of the body, including the five viscera (heart, liver, spleen, lungs, kidneys) and the "digestive system," including the stomach and intestines, will be touched on and stimulated. Therefore, there is a reason why practitioners of meditation are normally in good health and are able to maintain a healthy, radiant complexion. Indeed, I have seen several older practitioners who have returned to a youthful state.

My master once said: "If a practitioner is able to finally animate his true energy passing through all his channels, he will gain the purest and most ordered subtle energy in the universe. The microcosmic orbit enters into the macrocosmic orbit. At this time, most practitioners will feel that their sexual organs and genitals have been pulled back into the body, and slowly become strong, shrinking to be like those of a newborn child. Then, perhaps, the true breathing[127] will occur. You need to frequently bring your attention to the lower *dantian*. Continue practicing like this until you enter into the state of '*yin* and horse are mutually hidden.'"[128]

---

127 真息 (*zhenxi*). Literally, "true breathing." It is an advanced state of breathing similar to embryonic breathing. As this happens, the physical breathing process becomes increasingly more subtle, and then for periods of time may cease altogether.

128 馬陰藏相境界 (*Ma Yin Zang Xiang Jing Jie*). A sign of spiritual achievement, indicated by the shrinking of the male genitalia.

The master then proceeded, step by step, to recount and explain what he had received from the practice of meditation; and where it was related to the meditation practice, he also made mention of the eight extraordinary meridians. He mentioned that most people only focus on opening the conception and governing channels, when in actuality the other channels are also very important. According to some of the older practitioners of Qingcheng Mountain, if the micro- and macrocosmic orbits are opened, and the practitioner practices without interruption, he could live to the age of 100. But this is not an easy thing to accomplish. Our master once explained that even if a practitioner of great capacity wished to open up the microcosmic orbit he would have to practice meditation every day for a year before any small amount of achievement would occur.

In order to illustrate this, my master offered his personal experience: "Once, after I had only been studying for a short time, I was on the mountain with my teacher. As soon as I sat down, the *yang qi* came up from the area of my navel. Very often while doing this, I had the experience of feeling many bright spots. In the beginning there were only a few, but slowly the numbers increased and sometimes my whole body would glow like neon. I began to quite enjoy the feeling, but later when my master discovered this, he berated me. He explained that before certain medicines had been collected, experiencing these bright points or lights from the body is not actually a good sign. When I finally entered the state of heavenly circuit, I saw the lights again, but at this time I felt no happiness about it or attachment to it. I only maintained the practice and remained in a natural state. In this way, there were no dangers."

Generally speaking, these days, many people feel that opening a channel is a very simple matter. But when the channel is really open, you can often get the feeling that you are drinking a very old liqueur. You feel slightly drunk and numb; you are relaxed but uninhibited and cheerful. At this time there are no worries or obstructions in the mind. For some people, when this happens the *qi* flows quite strongly; a great amount of saliva is produced in the mouth and it will taste sweet like that of a baby. The most important thing to pay attention to is that when the *qi* crosses the top of the head, many people will experience tinnitus. They will often see subtle and obscured lights, and of course there will be many other phenomena.

CHAPTER **49**

THE LINK BETWEEN OPENING UP THE EIGHT CHANNELS AND THE BRAIN

At this point, the teacher circled back to an earlier topic: "Apart from the conception and governing channels, there are six others. How does one open all of these? If you are to open the eight channels, you must first root out the 'three disturbances' of the brain, abdomen, and feet. Only by doing this is it possible to open all of the channels. For example, if you are to open the conception and governing channels, you must cut off the disturbance at the back of the head. In our lineage, this is done with the complete set of the 'Eight Extraordinary Channel Practice,' and this is very effective. I have already passed this to you. You should practice this in your free time. Once the eight channels have been opened, a person will be happy and carefree throughout the entire day and will be free of misfortune and illness."

From a medical perspective, the pineal gland is quite a mysterious region of the brain. Many Western doctors and philosophers have spent a good part of their careers trying to understand it. They believe the pineal gland contains deep secrets concerning the human psyche. If more is discovered concerning the pineal and its degenerative process, a great connection between this and Daoist practices will be realized. The pineal gland has a direct effect on the immune system, skin tissue, the central nervous system, and the secretion of melatonin. These secretions have a strong influence on the mind, stamina, and emotions. The pineal gland and melatonin also play a large part in the aging process. Through meditation practice, one can impact the secretion of melatonin, to fight oxidation and remove free radicals. In this way, one can protect and maintain health on a cellular level.

"Currently, you are still young and have not yet reached 20 years of age. According to Daoist theory, your pineal gland has not begun to decline yet. In addition, your body has not begun to decline; you haven't lost energy, so there is no need to supplement. You can directly begin to practice Daoist alchemy. Once you reach 20 years of age—or at 17 or 18, for some who mature early—the reproductive organs start functioning as an adult. The best advice is to stick to the tradition and practice to the stage of 'yin and horse are mutually hidden,' and then begin to practice Daoist alchemy. When old, if the essence leaks out excessively, then practice until the yang qi is created again. Only then can you proceed further and practice 'yin and horse are mutually hidden.'

"For female practitioners, it is possible to practice Daoist alchemy before menstruation. Women who have yet to reach 49 years of age must first practice 'stopping the red dragon,' which halts menstruation, and only then continue to practice the Daoist foundational path. For those who have already reached menopause, it is necessary to first restart menstruation; then they must practice 'stopping the red dragon' and stop menstruation once more. So, there are many hurdles in the practice of meditation; it's not so simple.

"There are three critical barriers in the governing channel—one of the eight extraordinary channels—that must be passed through during the process leading up to the circulation of the micro- and macrocosmic orbits. In my experience, yuzhen (BL-9 acupuncture point) is the most difficult point to break through. Anyone with experience knows that breaking through this juncture is followed by a specific sound. In general, among the eight extraordinary channels, the yinqiao is more easily passed through, while the daimai is more difficult. So, when meeting a group of married men past the prime of life who wished to practice, I instructed them to start with the yinqiao. After they were able to break through, they could turn around and practice the governing and conception channels. This was a point of advice passed on to me from a senior practitioner of another sect. Right now, where you are in your practice, regardless of whether you follow an orthodox method or one that I have taught you, without circulating the qi, adjusting the breath, focusing on a point, or observing the mind, you can still enter directly into the stage of practice, the 'refinement of spirit back to emptiness.'"

This was what my teacher passed on to me. I carried out my practice accordingly. After practicing for about two weeks, I found that my strength and vigor had increased. My appetite doubled. My mind was extremely clear and my chest was open and clear. At times, I would read books until late but I wouldn't feel exhausted nor would my eyes become sore or swollen. The most miraculous thing was that, although my appetite had increased, my weight didn't change and I didn't become fat. On the contrary, I became much more lean and muscular. In short, both my strength and vigor greatly increased.

CHAPTER 50

A Deep Connection to Hua Mountain and Hearing the Legend of Patriarch Chen Tuan

One day, the woman who helped to prepare the master's meals called me and asked me to visit the master over the weekend. Naturally, I complied with her request. When I arrived, I found the master conversing with several of the older villagers. When he noticed me, he gestured for me to wait for him in the large hall. A couple of hours later, after the master had seen his guests out, he returned to the seat that he would commonly be found sitting on. He called me over to the front of his couch and spoke to me: "When I was young, I was very interested in this practice of the cosmic orbit. At my home, several times I listened to a certain scholar speaking on the *Yi Jing*. While attending talks at his home, I heard the honored name of Patriarch Chen Tuan mentioned. His full name was Chen Xiyi. Strangely, it seemed that there was some kind of karmic connection, and I began to feel admiration for the Daoist path. Later, I went to Qingcheng Mountain and followed my karmic connection. In my master's lineage, Chen Tuan was the most important lineage master. At one time, my master sent me to Hua Mountain to take the ritual precepts. On that trip, I took the long-anticipated opportunity to visit and pay my respects to the cave where lineage master Chen Tuan had achieved in his sleeping practice. There was an exquisite cave in a natural setting near the Jade Spring Court. The interior was not very large, and inside, in a reclining position, was his likeness on an altar. I even meditated in front of that cave for a bit, hoping to experience some sort of correspondence. Strangely enough, I ended up sitting there from

1pm until 5am or 6am the next morning, when I was disturbed from my deep, blissful trance by a large group of mice at first light. I felt at that time that only a moment had passed. I hadn't realized that I had spent the entire night there. From this experience, I got the feeling that I was learning directly from the master himself.

"On this visit to Hua Mountain it came about that I met a fellow practitioner, the Daoist priest Yi Yangzi. After he had introduced himself, he told me that all the patriarchs of his lineage had practiced the 'Hibernating Dragon Practice,' which had been passed down through the Chen Tuan lineage. Chen Tuan had been a Daoist monk on that mountain. It was Chen Tuan's destiny to visit this mountain to the cloud bower in the year 947 CE. During the time he spent on Hua Mountain, he was able to do the reclining practice. As a result, sometimes, upon lying down he would sleep for several months without getting up. Indeed, once while he was strolling through an old forest, where the canopy seemed to reach the sky, he suddenly lay down in the middle of the path and went to sleep. After many days, a cart passed by. The horse stumbled over the body of the sleeping Chen Tuan, who had been completely covered with leaves by this point. The cart was overturned; however, Chen Tuan was completely unaware of it.

"From childhood, Chen Tuan had been proficient in the 'Practice of the Heavenly Circuit,' and he also had an outstanding natural intelligence and sensibility. There was a man, surnamed Cao, who in the Song dynasty was to become a great general. Chen Tuan looked at him and told him: 'You have a noble appearance, but it's a shame that you won't live a long life. I hope that in the days to come, when you become an official and serve the people, you will be able to bring wellbeing to others in order to compensate.' Later on, General Cao[129] achieved a very high social status, as was expected. Furthermore, he believed in the words of Chen Tuan even more. Therefore, whenever he approached a battlefield, he would first sternly warn his officers against any acts of rape, pillaging, or the harming of innocent people. Once, in order to avoid killing, he made efforts to come up with an alternative solution rather than

129 General Cao Cao, mentioned previously in Chapter 18.

going into battle in order to further his career. On another occasion, in order to avoid taking up his post, he pleaded illness and reported to the messenger: 'My illness is not the kind which can be resolved by taking medicine.' Because these soldiers and General Cao had, over the years, been through many dangers together, they all made vows to capture the enemy whenever possible and never to harm the innocent. Later on, in an area south of the River Yangtze, they won a battle. From the day that they entered the city that had fallen to them, they not only respected the lives of the innocent, letting no harm come to them, but they also won over the hearts of the citizens living there. In this way they were able to maintain control over the more than 10,000 citizens living there.

"After this happened, Chen Tuan met General Cao again. Chen Tuan astonishingly told him: 'How strange it is that after not having seen you for a period, your whole appearance has changed.' General Cao asked Chen Tuan: 'May I ask, good sir, where the difference is?' Chen Tuan told him: 'To be honest, I thought you had died a long time ago. I hadn't imagined that you would have accumulated so many good deeds. This I can see in the lines on your face. And your lifespan seems to have strangely lengthened, which is apparent from the hairs around your ears. Your face is bright like the rays of the sun in the morning. It seems that in this period of time you have accumulated a great deal of merit. Now it looks like you could make it to the heaven of limitless blessings, as well as adding several years to your lifespan.' Later, his progeny became a great pillar of society, dedicated to the betterment of his country. What is more, this general did not meet with an early death. From this we can see that your appearance can change depending on the state of your mind. And taking up the performance of good deeds is a reasonable undertaking to dedicate oneself to."

Zhao Kuangyin, the founder of the Song dynasty, also had an uncanny relationship with Chen Tuan. The end of the Tang dynasty was not a peaceful time, and many people had no means of livelihood. Zhao Kuangyin took military action, and after Chen Tuan found out about this, he happily exclaimed: "From this day on, the conditions are already settled. The future is already decided." Zhao had invited Chen Tuan to become an official in his court, but Chen Tuan always had a reason to decline. Zhao was never willing to give up, to the point where he once wrote a request in the form of a poem to Chen Tuan:

The white cloud emerged during the previous court[130]
Before disappearing without a trace,
Assuming that your consent to the appointment is given,
I would beg the three summits to accompany thou.[131]

From this poem you can see the eagerness with which Zhao was seeking worthy men. Ultimately, Chen Tuan was unable to resist Emperor Zhao's persistence and finally came down from his mountain, escorted by one of the many messengers sent to him. The emperor made every effort to entertain Chen Tuan and make him feel satisfied with his position. But Chen Tuan was very clear about how the emperor had obtained his throne. He saw that living with the emperor was like living with a tiger, and he was very clear about the philosophy of "casting aside the bow once all the birds have been shot." However, in a situation where circumstances are greater than the individual, Chen Tuan could do nothing but force himself to comply in order to avoid a difficult situation. In the end, when they met face to face, Chen Tuan gave Emperor Zhao a few sincere words of advice: "You must seek out the greatest scholars and invite them to join you, regardless of how far away they are. Distance yourself from flattering ministers, reduce taxes on the people, and for those talented generals, give them the greatest reward and encouragement." The emperor tried to entice him to stay but to no avail. He even organized a special ceremony for him and conferred upon him the respectful title of "Mr Xi Yi."

For later scholars of the *Yi Jing*, Chen Tuan has a very important position, especially regards his collected writings, *Illustrations of the Heavenly Circuit* and *Map of the Unmanifested Aspects of the Dao*. He had a great influence on the Confucian thought of the

---

130 The emperor of the Later Zhou conferred upon Chen Tuan the honorary title "Master White Cloud" as Chen Tuan had been practicing at the Cloud Terrace Monastery.

131 Indicating the upper echelon position the emperor was willing to appoint Chen Tuan to. Poetically speaking, the emperor here was telling Chen Tuan he would go as far to move the mountains for him (the cloud) to abide 一曾向前朝出白雲, 後來消息杳無聞, 如今若肯隨微召, 總把三峰乞與君一.

Song, Yuan, and Ming dynasties. In addition, he conducted a very deep study into Daoism, Confucianism, and the practices of immortality. In this way, he generated works that his predecessors could not have conceived of. He was a rare and unique force and an academic leader.

Chen Tuan lived at the cloud bower on Hua Mountain for about 40 years altogether. During this time, there was an endless stream of practitioners coming from all directions with requests for instructions on the path of practice. For this reason, Patriarch Chen Tuan is considered to be a very important lineage holder in China's Daoist tradition.

CHAPTER **51**

THE ART OF SLEEPING WELL

My master told me about the year he went to Hua Mountain. This included stories about Daoist practitioners he met there and the events that transpired. In the end, he impressed upon me how fortunate he was to meet an old practitioner of Chen Tuan's practice method. It was from him that my master received Chen Tuan's 32-character oral instruction. At the time that he was getting this instruction, he had already been practicing for a long while, but still had not been able to find his way in the practice. He went around Hua Mountain asking politely for help. He inquired of three different Daoist priests the details of the 'Hibernating Dragon Practice,' and because of this he was slowly able to enter into the right conditions for practice. My master once told me: "The most important thing is this: You have to focus your mind and spirit on the *dantian* and combine the mind and breath into one. The heart and the kidneys must be in accord, and the mind cannot be allowed to wander. Then the *qi* can naturally abide. Before you close your eyes, you have to collect the mind and expel delusions. In this way, the *qi* will move naturally on its path, the breath will come and go naturally, and finally you will enter into the state of turtle breathing."

My master also explained all of the sleeping postures that had been explained to him by Daoist practitioners that year. However, he said after listening to them, it seemed there were two or three different ways to explain them. But basically, in all of the postures, the practitioner was to lie on his side and use one bent arm as a pillow. The other hand would be on the lower abdomen at the position of the *dantian*. One leg would be pulled in while the other one would be stretched out. It is just like the posture of a dragon curled up—therefore, it is called the sleeping dragon practice. My master said that, as he had been using this method of practice for a period of time, he had the experience that all these practices were heading in the same direction.

So to sum up, if your breath is joined and unified with the mind, the mind will be steady. If you can do this, you will, whether you are moving, still/abiding, sitting, or reclining, be in the state of listening while being deaf, having eyes but being blind, being mute and silent of mind, breathing without breathing, and moving without moving. If you use this method at all times, your spirit will very naturally become full, you will no longer find yourself wrestling with simply falling asleep in the practice, and after a time you will very naturally enter into the path of the Dao.

My master had already taught me a form of sleeping practice. He explained: "Sleep on your side, with your left hand under your chin and your right hand on your kidneys. Your left leg should be bent in and your right one should be stretched downward. Keep your attention on the *dantian*, and maintain an awareness of your breath. Begin by counting your breaths up to 10; then slowly increase to 100, 200, and finally all the way up to 360. Practice slowly until the same *yang* breathing that you get in meditation comes about, then enter into the practice of the micro- and macrocosmic orbits. You will experience many states in the process of this practice. Therefore, you will need to find a practitioner with experience to guide you."

While I was learning this, my master also told me of the differences in the experiences he had had while studying in the School of Complete Reality and the Hua Mountain School. However, he added that because he had started his preliminary training at Qingcheng Mountain, he still regards the Dragon Gate Sect of the School of Complete Reality as his lineage.

At the time, he also recited for me from the Qiu Changchun Immortal Dragon's Gate School placard. He wanted me to keep this in mind, and then he gave my my monastic name:

Zhen chang shou tai qing.

Yi yang lai fu ben.

He jiao yong yuan ming.

Zhi li zong cheng xin.

Chong gao si fa xing.

Shi jing rong wei mao.

Xi wei yan zi ning.

These are the first eight sentences. All together there are 2,100 characters. But if you are not a disciple of that lineage, they will be meaningless to you. I'm only telling you to help you understand about the Confucian traditions of China. You must never forget your origins.

CHAPTER **52**

TWELVE LIFE-SAVING
POSTING METHODS

During this transmission, *Sifu* was very compassionate and instructed me in *hunyuanzhuang* (a posting practice), as well as Taiji, *Xingyi* and *Baguazhang* (the three main martial art forms of the Wudang style). During those years, he often traveled to the Taiqing temple to seek out a Daoist master named Zhou, who was a very accomplished practitioner. He had a high level of skill in the practice of internal alchemy, Traditional Chinese Medicine, and herbal medicine. Anytime *sifu* could find some free time, he would immediately go to the Houshan district of Taipei to seek out this fellow practitioner. All told, this master taught *sifu* 12 forms of posting practice. Over time, *sifu* very generously passed all of these on to me. Thinking back on it, I can't help but shed tears of thankfulness. I can never forget the lightness and grace that he displayed at that time when teaching me, an imposing and elegant shape moving like a celestial immortal with the air of precepts coming from his Daoist robes. To this day I still feel that as I do my sitting and walking meditation practices he seems to be here tapping me to keep me awake.

Sifu had mentioned before, this set of posting practices could save a person's life and also give them a new lease on life. *Sifu* had said that among his past students, if someone had a mild stroke, if they were in the beginning stages of cancer, if they were having problems with their immune system or digestive system, or if they had high blood pressure, then seeing a doctor or taking medicine would be useless. But if they only practiced this form of *gongfu* for half an hour every day, there would always be a good result. While speaking, he would demonstrate the style: "First you must relax your whole body. When you have relaxed to the point that you cannot relax further and you feel that the body has slackened, allow the legs to naturally sink down into a slight squat. Don't let the knees extend beyond the big toes.

"Along with this, imagine yourself accepting the natural *qi* of the earth and allow it to flow up from the *yongquan* point directly to the lower *dantian*. At this point, once again relax the front of the hip a bit and allow the *qi* to flow directly up the spine. When it reaches the 'Great Hammer' acupoint (on the back of the neck) raise the arms as if hugging a tree or a large sphere. Tuck the chin in slightly toward the chest, keep the eyes half open and half closed, and focus on an area about one meter ahead. Breathe through the nose. On inhalation, roll the tongue up, pressing on the upper palate; on exhalation, roll the tongue down, pressing on the lower palate. Imagine the arms encircling a formless taiji ball (ball with the taiji symbol on it). This is the first style."

Master had great patience and would demonstrate while explaining and have me practice alongside him. Perhaps it was because I was young, but I quickly felt a current of warm *qi* coming from the 'Bubbling Well' point on the sole of my foot. It would flow up each calf, up the inside of the thighs and reach the *dantain*. It would then come from the hips through the sacrum, and rush up to the 'Jade' pressure point (on the back of the head).

It was actually quite strange, but both arms would simply float up of their own accord. This was a real surprise and I immediately asked my master about this. I was told to not give it any attention and to simply keep standing, following the method.

CHAPTER 53

TRANSMISSION AND GUIDANCE FROM THE MASTER

Sifu instructed me in these methods incrementally, following a step-by-step sequence which started from delving into the classics, the *Dao De Jing, Huang Ting Jing, Qing Jing Jing* and *San Tong Qi*, among others, which he explained and clarified. He also showed me how to apply these in meditation. As I had by then already familiarized myself with the fundamentals of classical Chinese, reading was no hard feat. However, at the initial stage, it is difficult to avoid feeling somewhat in the dark as I was unable to draw the connections to the terminology and applications found in Daoist scriptures.

For example, Daoists employ the regular use of such terms as "lead" and "mercury," and it was only later that I came to know that these refer to the *qi* and spirit, respectively. For instance, I once saw the phrase "cast mercury into a lead cave." If you don't know that this means you must unify the spirit and *qi*, leading the spirit into the *qi* while not allowing the *qi* to leak outward, then you will have no way of knowing how to practice. Some patriarchs excelled at using nature as imagery for the body—some used the sun to represent spirit and the moon as a metaphor for *qi*. For fear of the teaching falling into the wrong hands, some patriarchs went as far as to transmit their teachings through verse and odes. The divinatory trigrams from the *Yi Jing*—notably the *xunfeng* and *kunhuo*—were used by some. Unless it had been pointed out to you, you would have no way of understanding that the one refers to breath, while the other to *qi*.

As I reminisce, it becomes clear that the way people today buy books and blindly base their practice on them is very dangerous indeed. For instance, after meditating daily for six or seven hours, your whole body will start feeling very weak and flabby, as if you had a serious cold; sometimes you will feel ill-at-ease, unable to focus your will. If you don't have the guidance of an experienced teacher, you will not know that this is in actual fact the result of your meditation. When the *yang qi* emerges as a result of having received the impulse of *qi*, many people will ask themselves if they have not already fallen sick or if their practice has taken a wrong turn somewhere. This is a big misunderstanding. When the *yang qi* recedes, you will mostly feel happy and delighted in mind and body, as if all gloominess had been swept away in an instant; every day is like a new spring, self and things all forgotten, the mind free of all intoxication.

As a matter of fact, people who are approaching the stage of "gathering medicine" will indeed have this kind of experience. If you have no means of collecting and assimilating your thoughts, delusive thinking, doubts, worries, and fears, you might miss out on a great opportunity to accomplish something rare, and thus be unable to integrate your spirit and *qi*. However, some people might unwittingly see their vitality bloom as the *yang qi* bursts out from the *dantian*, but lacking the perspicacious gaze of a discerning eye, they squander this opportunity, at which point they are left with nothing but regret. How can we go a step further to unify the *qi* and essence, and use breathing methods to increase the inner heat, preventing the true *qi* from leaking outward? This process is what is known as "gathering the medicine and returning to the furnace."

Within each process, it is due to a knowledgeable guide that you will know when to use the breath, harmonize the true *qi*, and do this alongside the rising and lowering of the conception and governing channels. In terms of micro- and macrocosmic orbits, just one cycle of inhaling and exhaling alone is a vast area of study. Thus, if nobody explains the words of past masters, you would have no way of knowing that the *gan* trigram refers to the head, while the *kun* trigram refers to the abdomen. Also, you would be at a loss as to how to move and drive the *qi* inside by means of the breath.

What can be said of all these technical terms, such as "entering the yang fire,"[132] or "withdrawing the yin seal"?[133] What do they

---

132 進陽火 (*jinyanghuo*).
133 退陰符 (*tuiyinfu*).

mean? If someone were to explain to you in a few words how to breathe, from which place to "bring it upward" and at which point it "enters," how to grasp the fortunate timing and crucial moment, and also how to use the rising and lowering of the breath, only then would you be able to circulate the *qi* naturally. Moreover, the explanations of various sects differ in subtle ways. It is only after someone has explained things to you that you will realize: "Oh! These 'to draw out and replenish' and 'to raise and lower' are one and the same, and this rising and lowering also has its appropriate time and number of repetitions, according to inhalations and exhalations, and is not something which can be done arbitrarily." Here, *Sifu* clearly went over things once again: From what time to what time is referred to as "*yang* time." The movements you do at that time are referred to as "entering the *yang* fire." All movements performed during the period extending from 11am to 11pm are referred to as "withdrawing the yin seal." These times, as well as the early morning time from 5am to 7am, and the period from 5pm to 7pm in the early evening, are called the "four times" by Daoists.

Then, how to return to warming the *dantian*? Warming is actually just "bathing." *Sifu* explained with great clarity: "When the microcosmic orbit is just starting to move, many people will come to a halt. One must be careful at this point: How to allow it to circulate? You need a transmission from a qualified teacher, who explains at what moment you must elevate the fire, then lead it to become essence, and finally refine the essence into *qi*. At this point, a great, blooming energy appears, which you can circulate around the microcosmic orbit. In the fullness of time, the golden pill will be naturally created."

CHAPTER 54

TIPS ON MEDITATION
RETREAT AND FASTING

Every summer and winter, *sifu* would take a retreat lasting between 49 days to two months in an ancient temple in the mountains of Yuli, Hualien county. During the retreat, he would abstain from food for the entire time, only consuming liquids. On the few occasions I was attending to him during his retreat, *sifu* instructed me on how complex the Daoist fasting method was and how it shouldn't be taken lightly. For instance, before beginning to fast, one should gradually reduce daily food consumption from two meals to one meal a day, thus allowing the digestive system to adapt to the new regime. Then, slowly switch to only liquids, whilst paying attention to good nutrition. One of the liquids *sifu* regularly consumed during the retreat includes a drink mixed with ground pine nuts, peanuts, black beans, and other nuts that provide necessary minerals and nutrients. He would, however, only drink it once at midday and take only warm spring water for the rest of the day.

Sifu also explained how three days or a week before the fasting is due to be completed, and depending on how long the fasting period is, one should work one's way back up from liquids to slowly consuming light and soft food, increasing food intake from one meal to two meals a day, before returning to the normal routine. By doing so, practitioners can shield themselves from diseases associated with the digestive system and avoid internal bleeding. I followed the instructions and experimented a couple of times before I realized that sages of the past and Daoist immortals who put their body through the test of eradicating desire for food did so not just for the purpose of practicing austerities, but actualizing the Daoist principles of precepts, meditation, and wisdom. Indeed, the meditative joy derived after the fast significantly assisted my meditation.

While meditating in the mountains, one often experiences the oneness of nature, heaven, and humanity, which explains why most of the Daoist blessed spots can be found in many of the famous mountains in China. The aforementioned ancient temple in Yuli, Hualien county, is located in the east of the central mountain range of Taiwan. A sizable building with a vast open area lined with bamboos and cypress trees, the temple is a glistening paradise basking in early morning sunlight. Rich fragrance from various flowers and the aroma from the forest permeate the space, clearing the mind of the meditator and leading to better results. Behind it, a long, winding creek embraces the temple in the shape of a bent bow. When the end of summer approaches, a meandering trail by the temple is lined with tree leaves in the hue of splashing red—a magnificently delightful scene indeed! While standing on the top of the mountain looking down, the view of row upon row of mountain huts with their kitchen chimneys puffing smoke and their flickering lights dotted around the hills comes into sight, creating the ambience of an otherworldly realm reminiscent of Shangri La. The recollection of the scene brings warmth and comfort to me. It all seems like just yesterday.

CHAPTER 55

PROTECT, LOVE AND RESPECT LIFE

Every day before morning classes *sifu* would walk around the ancient paths and alleys surrounding the monastery. He would carry a bamboo basket and pick any herbs that he saw that he thought might be useful. Sometimes he would even find *xiancao* or grass jelly, *Echinops grijsii*, and *Anoectochilus formosanus*. *Sifu* also taught me how to identify and detoxify some medicinal herbs. It is said that in the mountains of Hualien there is such an abundance of valuable herbs that one could come across hundreds of species just on a casual walk. Due to *sifu's* mastery of Chinese Medicine and herbology, during this period of time I truly gained a vast amount of invaluable experience.

Once *sifu* was walking in the woods, when he saw a pair of birds. One was a young bird whose feathers hadn't fully grown in yet. Its mother was doing its best to take care of the chick since their nest had been destroyed. *Sifu* took this opportunity to tell me: "Go and fix their nest so that they'll have a proper dwelling." *Sifu* then proceeded to give an example from *The Treatise on Response and Retribution*, saying: "A bird's nest is its refuge. If we arbitrarily destroy it, then this is what's known as 'something people and the gods cannot tolerate.'"

Sifu told me: "Those of us who practice Daoism are the mothers and fathers of all souls and sentient beings and therefore we need to do our utmost to protect them. This nest is the birds' only safe haven, sheltering them from the wind and rain. If one were to destroy it, how would that be any different from a bandit burning down someone's home? If in this life you destroy a bird nest, break eggs, burn mountain forests, or pollute water, then in your next life you definitely won't have any children, grandchildren, or descendants; and those who make a living capturing birds will especially face negative retribution. Once when I was in Sichuan province I met a man named Chen who made a living capturing birds in the mountains and selling them at the market. Several years later I heard that while trying to catch a mother bird and its chick, he fell out of a tall tree and smashed his head on a rock. He suffered brain damage, causing damage to his five senses. This is surely a case of karmic retribution within one's lifetime. Heaven has the virtue of cherishing life, so you must always bear firmly in mind not to harm any living thing; whether mosquitoes, flies, bugs or animals you should do your best to protect them.

"If you think about why the unicorn is considered the most auspicious of all creatures, it's because it doesn't even trample on grass and therefore won't eat any insects. In fact, if you look at history, as long as there was a virtuous and kind monarch, one that loved the common people as their own children, or one that didn't arbitrarily kill sentient beings, then that country would give rise to a unicorn. If there were any killing of beings or the horrors of war, then a unicorn would assuredly not grace that area with its presence. Likewise, if people of a region catch fish for a living, gut animals, or harm sea creatures, then a dragon definitely won't manifest in that area. If a mountain region has lots of hunters destroying nests and taking eggs, then there's no chance a phoenix would dwell there. From this we can gather that even animals understand avoiding evil to prevent retribution, not to mention humans who have supremacy over all animals.

"Spiritual practice is not preserving one's integrity while ignoring others. In the School of Complete Reality we have always believed that obtaining the fruits of the practice depend on an accumulation of benevolent good deeds as a foundation. Even if you could sit in meditation for 10,000 years, if you have not accumulated this foundation, then you will not achieve; on the day of your death you will be held back. So, aside from meditation, it is important to study the deeds of saintly people, those great people whose stories of inspiring charisma were so magnificent as to be told far and wide. These complete the tools of a true Daoist practitioner."

CHAPTER 56

ESSENTIAL DIETARY GUIDELINES FOR MEDITATION

During my study with *sifu*, I was subtly influenced by his vegetarian diet. This had resulted in an aversion to the smell of meat that persisted for a couple of years. *Sifu* once instructed that if a practitioner wished to attain the highest state of meditative stillness, they must avoid meat, fish, and any pungent or stimulating foods. What he meant was that all meat is essentially impure. When one consumes impure foods, one's breathing will eventually become coarse. This is particularly true for meditators because meat consumption slows down the movement of *qi* and shortens both the inhalation and exhalation.

In addition, *sifu* also talked about how practitioners should avoid pungent foods such as chilies, garlic, onions, Chinese leeks and chives, etc. It is because consuming these pungent foods will disperse the condensed *qi* stored in the body. Daoist alchemists who are about to enter the stage of "gathering medicine" will fall short of success upon consuming pungent foods. This is the reason *sifu* kept a strict diet with great discipline. His daily staples included lightly cooked vegetables and rice with minimal seasoning, no sauce, and absolutely no processed foods. He rarely consumed starches, and would instruct those who cooked for him to use unrefined and handmade ingredients as often as possible.

Sifu further instructed: "Never overeat. Keep the stomach 30 percent full and nothing more, because overeating reduces the mind to drowsiness. For Daoist practitioners, overeating is the main cause of mental fatigue. It will significantly shorten the length of their meditation, stagnate the flow of *qi*, and clog important channels of the body. However, practitioners who are in the process of opening these channels should avoid being in the state of hunger or there will be insufficient heat in the body, which will block the rise of *yang qi*." I relished every opportunity to attend to *sifu* on his retreat, during which time I would frequently acquire unexpected experiences invaluable to my practice.

On one such occasion, *sifu* told me: "Since time immemorial, diets and medicinal substances have played a crucial part for any truth-seeking Daoist practitioners before they could cultivate the golden pill. Daoism has always been an integral part of spiritual practice for the Chinese. From the Wei, Jin and North–South dynasties (220–589 CE) onward, members of the aristocracy and literati alike would seek out masters and sages from whom they hoped to uncover the secret of immortality. The School of Complete Reality of Daoism has produced generations of Daoist spiritual masters who, since the last millennium, had passed on their invaluable experiences of maintaining good health through the use of herbs and minerals. Take the extracting of 'Solomon's seal,' which involves the painstaking methods of nine rounds of steaming and sun-drying cycles. According to the Chinese *Materia Medica*, the benefits of frequent use of Solomon's seal include a youthful complexion that is wrinkle-free. It's also a natural appetite suppressant. In addition, Solomon's seal has a healing effect on physical fatigue and mental weakness by supplementing the kidney *qi*. When taken properly, meditators will reap enormous benefits during the stage where they work to transform essence into *qi*. Additionally, Solomon's seal can be taken alone as a single herb without the guiding herbs to assist its assimilation into the body. It substantially benefits the spleen and the lungs as well as those who suffer from lower back pain and cannot sit for a long time. Furthermore, regular consumption is of great benefit for those with hyperlipidemia due to its blood-cleansing properties. Benefits will accumulate for those suffering from hyperalimentation, fatty liver, and tuberculosis. I personally take this prior to fasting as it does a fine job in suppressing appetite.

"Pine nuts and Chinese arborvitae are also an integral part of the fasting diet of Daoist practitioners. Chinese arborvitae is greatly beneficial to meditators and Daoist alchemists due to nourishing properties that soothe the internal organs. While taking a retreat in the mountains where humidity is inevitable, practitioners are able to reap the benefits of regular consumption of Chinese arborvitae because it helps to clear humidity and protect from common colds as well as open up the acupoints. Again, it's a natural appetite suppressant. Those who regularly consume it will not feel lethargic but physically and mentally light and relaxed. Asparagus is another herb that benefits people with a weak constitution and those who find it hard to sit for too long due to a lack of kidney *qi*."

All in all, I learned a lot about Daoist fasting methods during the time I studied with *sifu*. I learned to recognize and study over 100 medicinal herbs. However, as *sifu* had pointed out, it is of paramount importance that one has a teacher when learning the various methods of making herbal ointments, powder, or pills the size of parasol tree seeds. One needs to learn the entire process of making these herbal medicines because if one makes even just one mistake in a single sequence, the result can be hazardous and put one's life at risk.

CHAPTER 57

THE IMPORTANCE OF DRINKING WATER TO CULTIVATE HEALTH

From the age of ten, my teacher began spending long periods of time living in different mountain communities as well as in retreat. In those places, he followed many high-level Daoists from whom he learned effective methods to cultivate his physical health.

This is what he shared with me: "Water is formless medicine for those who practice the Dao. Water is the blood of the earth. Upon entering the throat, it becomes a wonderful drug that moistens the passageways. Not only can water cleanse the dirty and rotten parts of the body, it can also provide the entire body with necessary trace elements."

Sifu also said that in the past, while he was in the Qingcheng and Huashan mountains, he encountered many experienced Daoist elders. They explained to him how to cultivate his body through drinking water as well as how to locate mountain springs and the sources of water. After drinking from these natural sources, stones won't be produced in the body. However, as some of these mountain springs pass through mineral rocks, they carry high amounts of minerals. So, if you were to drink too long from these springs, stones in the body would more easily develop.

In addition to discussing the drinking of water, the elders also paid particular attention to the vessel used and what foods you should avoid after drinking water. A special point to note is that, during the day, before sunrise, you should face east to gather water. Some would even consult the *Farmers' Almanac* to pick auspicious days to begin drinking water.

My teacher taught me a mantra to recite while drinking water. He explained to me how to use it to cultivate *qi* and regulate my body. These methods have actually been transmitted from ancient times to the present. After the Tang and Song periods, many Daoist practitioners were influenced by the alchemy classics written by Wei Boyang, and many Daoist practitioners sought out the inner alchemy practice methods. The skill to cure illnesses with water gradually declined and was only passed on orally through certain teachers.

My teacher relayed a story to me of a time when he lived in the temple at Qingcheng Mountain where he encountered an alchemist, an elder Daoist renunciate. He guided my teacher through the water drinking breathing method, which includes breath retention and comes from the turtle breathing method. The main feature is taking in all of the *qi* into the *dantian*, and exhaling through both nostrils. Gradually, the amount of air that is exhaled will be reduced, while the air that is inhaled becomes greater. If you follow this method, you will start to feel that a portion of your *qi* in your lower abdomen starts to vibrate. This means that you will soon have accomplished the art of embryonic breathing.

Sifu mentioned the alchemist Mr. Zhao. He said that, from the time he was young, he would go up to the mountains and practice in a thatched shed. He would do this twice a year, either in the spring or the summer. My teacher said: "This man would only wear one set of clothes, consisting of a short gown and a thin shirt, even when there was snow and ice covering the ground. In his body, he collected hot *qi*. I would often go to his shed and see that it was almost completely empty. Other than his classical Daoist scripture, he only had a mat to sit on."

At one point, my teacher asked him in what manner he slept. The Daoist monk replied that he had not lain down to sleep for more than 30 years. My teacher thought this was a joke, so he decided to observe him during the night. He would never have expected what he found. This monk didn't breathe through his nose or mouth at all throughout the night. The only thing that he noticed was that the monk's abdomen would slightly tremble. This method is known as "turtle breathing" and it has been passed down through the generations throughout the world for a very long time.

CHAPTER 58

HEALTH CULTIVATION METHODS TO PRACTICE JUST BEFORE SLEEPING

Sifu said that, for a few years, he was greatly interested in the teachings of a Daoist elder named Zhao. At this time, *sifu* was still young. In addition, he was very respectful and sincere to others. For these reasons, he was well liked by all of the village elders on the mountain.

At one point, the Daoist elder named Zhao said to my teacher: "Right now, you are young and full of vigor. It's not suitable for you to immediately lie down when going to sleep. I'll give you a different method. Every night, when you are about to go to bed, your body needs to be in the shape of the character 大. Your body, mind, and extremities need to be relaxed. Hold your thumbs in your hands as if you were making a fist, and place them next to your thighs. Then, you have to breathe in and out in a relaxed manner. When you breathe in, your tongue needs to go up and rest behind your upper teeth. When you breathe out, your tongue should go down and curl up behind your bottom teeth. Gradually speed up the movement of your tongue as you swirl it inside your mouth. While doing this, you don't need to pay attention to your breathing; instead, just wait until your mouth fills up with saliva. When this happens, you need to close your mouth, aligning your upper and lower teeth with each other. Then, slowly swallow your saliva, while visualizing it going down as far as your *dantian*. As you are doing this, you must intentionally guide it down along with your breath from your nose. Then, take a short breath and hold it. Once you can't hold it any longer, let your breath slowly and gently exit from your mouth. This shouldn't be done too fast; you must let it out gradually. Finally, you can gently breathe in again. Repeat this process a few times, and make sure to stay relaxed."

Sifu continued: "If you can gradually increase the length of the retention, the '100 illnesses' can be averted, and you can live a long life. If, at a later point, you meet others with whom you have a karmic connection who wish to learn this method, you yourself must orally instruct them how to do this. In this way, you can prevent them from making errors, and therefore, you can make sure the correct method has been transmitted."

During the time that I was following my teacher, on many occasions he would instruct me on the methods from such classics as *The Most High Jade Scripture on the Internal View of the Yellow Court* and *The Most High Jade Scripture on the External View of the Yellow Court*. He would also instruct me on the Daoist *Treatise on Jade Calligraphy* and the *The Token for the Agreement of the Three According to the Yi Jing*, as well as the oral instructions for entering the Dao according to this book. When we had spare time, my teacher would also explain the teachings of Lu Chunyang in the *Bai Zi Ming* as well as Zhong Liquan's *The Jade Emperor's Heart-Mind Imprint Sutra*. I learned a great deal from all of these.

CHAPTER 59

LIVING IN MUNDANE AFFAIRS WITHOUT BEING TAINTED

This Is Curbing One's Mind

Sifu once explained: "In the future, due to the growth of commerce and technology, many people will find themselves sitting or lying down for long periods of time. Because of this, a great deal of diseases brought about through social situations involving drinking, smoking, and stress will arise, causing problems with eating and sleep. Young people like yourselves have the good connections to enter onto this rare path, but in the future this will be much more difficult. In the future you should have the connections to pass this on. Do not cut off your practice. Practicing the pill of immortality, simply put, has two paths—the quick path and the progressive path. Most modern people are excessively busy. Putting aside half an hour a day for meditation is already a struggle. The fast path is certainly out of reach when practicing like this. I have taught a lot of people in these ten years, but until today I have not met a single one who has been able to ask for all of my knowledge and all I can teach.

"In the past, when we went to the mountains to accompany my master in his practices, he would only share one practice with us. Generally, we would retreat for one week. This was to see whether or not we would be able to appreciate and realize the practice that our master would share.

"In the afternoon of each day our teacher would ask if there were any problems with the practice. After that, we would just practice according to the instructions. We would stay in the state of meditation throughout the day, undisturbed by any worldly affairs.

"How could modern people have this kind of free time? Knowing this, my teachings would mainly focus on the 'mind' aspect. Regardless of what the practice is, the focus should be on the transformation of the mind, which is the master of the spirit. If the mind is busy, the body will not be in a good state; there will be many distractions. How would it be possible to reach the final stages of practice of absorbing the spirit? The only way is to have the mind abide peacefully. Only then will the spirit coalesce."

There are quite a lot of practice methods available nowadays. Unfortunately most of them are unreliable. A while ago an older gentleman who had been dabbling in Daoist practices for a while came to visit me and asked about a specific practice called 'Knocking on the Bamboo to Call out the Turtle.' He spoke many things about his path of practice. After I had listened for a while, I asked him which teacher it was that taught him. He told me about how much money he spent, how many teachers he went to see, all in order to get this practice and return to his original youth. The 'knocking on bamboo' is waking up the vitality that has deteriorated. The 'bamboo' mentioned here is going through the perineum and the area of the prostate to get at the bundle of nerves at the deteriorated spinal column.

So many older practitioners didn't enter the path until past the age of 70. Most would use this method to first elevate and get back their original essence and original *qi* and compensate for excessive loss of energy from the *dantian*. The 'calling out the turtle' mentioned here, refers to once again bringing up the *yang qi* in order to raise the head of the turtle. The hidden meaning of the turtle here is a reference to the sexual organ of the man. In the past many accomplished southern practitioners gave quite thorough descriptions of this practice of striking the bamboo to wake the turtle. In the past, the accomplished practitioner Zhang also didn't meet with the path until a very late age—he used this practice as well. But this was certainly not the practice this person was talking about now, where he would just indiscriminately massage himself, rubbing so many times in a clockwise and then counterclockwise direction. I had actually never heard of this practice in the past.

There were many times in the past when my teacher would give a thorough explanation of the Daoist *Song of the Rootless Tree* by Grand Master Zhang Sanfeng. There is also a clear explanation of the aforementioned practice in the *Essays on Harmony*. There are currently very few people who understand the true meaning of this practice method. One ought to seek out wise people to ask. One can't just simply follow a baseless clue—this can be dangerous.

As for some secret practices, it will be enough to simply acknowledge that they exist. There's no need to practice them. Practice without steely determination can easily lead a person down the wrong path. One ought to be cautious. The purpose of adjusting and guarding the mind is to draw in the spirit and *qi* as well as to harmonize and nurture your internal organs. By so doing, over the course of time, the spirit and *qi* will be sufficient, joints supple, and essence replenished.

A practitioner of Daoism must first learn to conserve the mind and reduce mental grasping. When the mind is settled, everything else will be perceived as stable. Eventually the inner luminosity shines forth and that is the accomplishment of the Dao. The highest sign of collecting your mind is to live in the world without being tainted by it. The practice of "emptiness" is but a process of achieving Dao. In other words, true meditation is not sitting at the time of sitting, but sitting at all times. Sit until the spirit becomes like a mirror, this is the accomplishment of Dao.

CHAPTER 60

MEDITATION AND POSTING COMPLEMENTING ONE ANOTHER

During this time, *sifu* gave instruction on the keys of posting, which struck a chord with a lot of like-minded people in the *qigong* community. *Sifu* once recounted his encounter with a *Yiquan* expert in China and how this person advanced his skills through posting. He once emitted *qi* while posting, and by doing so, he created an invisible barrier with a 3-meter radius, through which no one could come. Those who tried were forced back by the *qi*. He was once challenged by a grand master of the schools of *Xingyi* and *Bagua*. To this grand master's great surprise, he was unable to get close to the *Yiquan* expert. Every strike he made was met by the *qi* barrier, which subsequently made the grand master stumble backward a couple meters and fall. *Sifu* not only was an acquaintance of this *Yiquan* expert but also held him in high regard, having exchanged experiences on the subject with him. In fact, the core principles of posting share the same source. For decades, *sifu* had made posting part of his daily practice and never went a day without doing it.

Within the dozen or so years that I followed *sifu*, I came to realize that mind is the master of essence, *qi*, and spirit. If the mind is clear and empty, then all practices will be perfectly accomplished. Early Daoist practitioners, drawing inspiration from their daily routine, invented a lot of exercises and practices to assist their main practice, while at the same time enhancing their understanding of the ultimate truth on the spiritual path.

Daoist exercises such as the "Eight-Section Brocade," "Twelve-Section Brocade," "Five Animal Exercise" and the "Tendon Changing Classic" are all employed as an extension of sitting meditation. This is because through the movement and techniques in these exercises, topped with focused attention and breathing, one can achieve the same result as from meditation. According to *sifu*, if a practitioner only relies on sitting meditation without other supplementary exercises to strengthen the tendons and muscles and boost blood and *qi* circulation, their body may stagnate like a pool of water and they may inadvertently harm themselves.

Beginners who sit for an extended period of time may suffer from stagnant *qi* below the waist. Posting at this stage can supplement their meditation by regulating the flow of *qi* and complement the essence and spirit. Based on the principles of moving and stillness, *yin* and *yang*, ancient sages invented these exercises to complement their meditation practice. *Sifu* took great pains to summarize the key points and once again illustrate and demonstrate the correct posting method: "To start, walk in place as if you are taking a leisurely walk. This helps regulate your mind and breath. Do it until the breath is fine and long. Once this is achieved, and your body and mind are both relaxed, feel as though your breath, fine and gentle, is the only thing that exists in the world at this moment and imagine a warm cloud of *qi* permeating the sky. From the space above you a fine drizzle falls onto your hair and enters and washes your body, purifying it with the five vital elements, namely earth, water, fire, air, and space. The rain falls onto the skin, penetrating the dermis and subcutaneous tissues and gradually reaching the fasciae and muscle. The rain also purifies all the nerve cells, revitalizing the withering, aging, and broken cells. It also purifies all internal organs, including the heart, brain, spleen, kidneys, lungs, stomach, and spine. You should feel your spirit invigorated and renewed after this visualization.

"You then stand with feet shoulder-width apart. Bend the knees slightly, as if they are gently pulled down by gravity. Make sure your knees don't extend past the toes. Gently bring your awareness to the *yongquan* acupoint at the soles of both feet. Relax, and while you are fully relaxed you will feel a surge of warmth bubbling up through the *yongquan* point and rising rapidly to the waist area between the kidneys. With the rise of the warm current, the arms rise simultaneously, forming a circle as if holding a tree. At this point, relax the body once more before mindfully regulating your breath. Count from 1 to 10 and from 10 to 1. Repeat ten times.

"While posting, focus your attention on the lower *dantian*. Visualize that everything you hear is melding with the *dantian*. With each out-breath, visualize all the illness and worries expelled from the body. Next, visualize the body emptying layer by layer, both inside and outside. If the concept of emptiness eludes you, you may simply allow your focused attention to provide the impetus to relax by visualising part of the body relaxing. Start from the skin and work your way in until the only thing left is the heart."

Based on my previous experiences, those who have a natural capacity for this would sometimes have a warming sensation in their *dantian*. To this, *sifu* would say that maintaining a natural state regardless of the sensation is key, with attention paid to any physical reaction and changes. Unlike meditation, one should avoid directing one's *qi* with intention while posting. When you feel the *qi* starting to tremble uncontrollably, open your eyes wide and stare into the sky. According to *sifu*, at the early stage of his posting practice, he would often be distracted by certain physical reactions and trembling *qi*. Not knowing what to do, he would consult his own *sifu* and through his guidance all of the aforementioned conditions disappeared.

CHAPTER **61**

THE WONDROUS PRACTICE COMBINING BREATH AND MANTRA

Sifu told me that, ideally, meditation and posting should be practiced during *yang* times, for at these times we will be almost devoid of thoughts of lust. It is the best time for promoting the *yang qi*. At the time, Master Tai also taught *sifu* a mantra. *Sifu* spoke of this mantra, mentioning that before you recite it you must click your teeth three times. *Sifu* said: "In retrospect, I came to believe that these mantras have their reason for being, especially in terms of calming the body and mind."

Many Daoist practitioners only know of refining the essence and transforming it into *qi*, and accumulating *qi* to make it become spirit, but very few pay attention to the means of guarding the three immortal souls and seven mortal souls that live within one's physical body. If you understand how to take advantage of the times when these aspects of the self are strongest, and meditate at these times, you will very naturally reap twice the benefit for half the effort in your cultivation. So, *sifu* considered that joining mantra recitation to one's breath could actually help one to control the movement of the *qi* and spirit in the physical body, something he found truly marvelous.

Sifu presented to me, in a simple manner, all the knowledge he had accumulated: how to drive the *qi* by means of the spirit when posting, with *mudras*; how to use one's fingers to tap, press, pinch, pull, and rub certain acupoints on the body, combining this with inhalation and exhalation; when to faintly inhale past some acupuncture point, and then disseminate the *qi* to another point; how to turn the original *qi* and true essence into true *qi*; how to practice with the micro- and macrocosmic orbits; and how to move around the "three gates" and all acupoints. Also, how to direct the saliva into the lower *dantian* by means of the conception channel, how to harmonize the *yin* and *yang* and bring the conception and governing channels together, as well as how to make it so there is no conflict. This is the School of Complete Reality's uncommon practice of "cleansing the marrow." What a pity that this method is gradually being lost. A number of years back, I met five or six Daoist priests from Qingcheng Mountain in Sichuan who were on a visit to Taiwan in order to attend the International Daoist Conference. As we chatted, I asked them about this practice, and to my surprise I just saw them looking at each other in dismay. They then shook their heads and said they had never heard of it.

Sifu had formerly learnt many types of posting and breathing methods from Master Tai. These breathing methods were further separated into "outer" and "inner." Other instructions included how to use true intention to lead the *qi*, assemble the *qi* and drive it, how to cultivate the *qi* by agitating it, and by means of the length or brevity of each breath and the number of breaths. For these to be of any assistance, they must be received orally and taken to heart. Through the guidance of a knowing teacher, you will little by little be able to enter into the state of extreme emptiness and earnest stillness. Most people are not privy to the fact that from a Traditional Chinese Medicine perspective, in our bodies, the heart, lungs, and liver are intolerant of excess heat, whereas the spleen, digestive tract, and kidneys must absolutely remain warm, neither too cold nor too dry. Through the practice of sitting meditation and posting, if you can cultivate the pre- and postnatal *qi* simultaneously and jointly enhance both your nature and life, you will naturally come to understand the sense behind the adage "When a chance arises, act on it; when there is no chance, do not practice." If you post for a very long time, you will eventually reap what is termed the "three flowering and gathering at the top and the five *qi* becoming the original *qi*" which refers to the transformation of essence and *qi* to spirit and the five vital breaths. However, these methods have been concealed across the famous mountains of China, or else have little by little waned and disappeared owing to the narrow-mindedness of selfish minds.

Sifu had a pillow which had a layer of porous, brown cloth wrapped around it; and around that was a somewhat oversized finely woven wicker case. I once asked out of curiosity: "*Sifu*, why do you change the content of this case every year?"

Sifu answered with a laugh: "This is a method that I acquired from my respected master when we were up in the mountains. Why do I use this medicinal pillow? At the time, my venerable master had told me that if you can assist your cultivation through some physical tools, and harmonize the *yin* and the *yang qi*, it will help in your cultivation. The most vital part of the human soul is concentrated at the crown of the head, and the head is where the greater part of the essence and blood is stored. Thus, such use of medicinal paste reaps unimaginable wonders as far as our physical body is concerned.

"On the rear side of Qingcheng Mountain live some Daoist practitioners over 100 years of age, whose grey hair has turned black and whose missing teeth have come through again. There are none for whom this is not linked to the joint practice of sitting meditation, posting, and this pillow. In those days, I would take this pillow and medicinal case along wherever I went. The way to make these, the types and doses of medicine used, the way to seal the pillow, or how long before you must renew it, were all imparted to me orally. I don't know if it helps in any way, but it is very clear that as long as I have slept on this pillow, I have not once had any dreams. Moreover, it indeed has a very noticeable effect on the circulation of *qi* and blood."

CHAPTER 62

THINGS TO TAKE NOTE
OF WHILE POSTING

Finally, *sifu* explained things to me in a way more accessible to the modern individual. When posting, do not let the mind disperse outward; then will the *qi* penetrate the *dantian*. If the mind is all over the place, the *qi* can by no means become pure and clear. The breathing cannot be disorderly, it must first be adjusted so that it is fine and delicate. The mind and the *qi* must become one, and then it can be led down below the navel. Lastly, concentrate fully on the lower *dantian*. Once the mind is able to focus below the navel, start little by little, to empty the mind. Ultimately, the *qi* and breath will follow their natural course: What ought to move will move, and what ought to stop will stop, without further need for interference. Whether a beginner or an old hand, this is one of the safest methods for posting.

Sifu also told us about a few points you must pay attention to in the initial stages of posting. He said: "When starting your practice, it is best if you can go by the adage of 'more posting sessions of shorter duration.' At the least, post three times a day, and no longer than ten minutes each time, then, gradually increase the time until you reach a half-hour per session. Any session below ten minutes will not really be worthwhile. It is appropriate to post only a half-hour to an hour after meals, and it should not be done on an empty stomach. During the summer, it is best to post on a spot of grass so as to absorb the *qi* of the earth. As you post, you can 'move' the *qi*, starting from the *yongquan* points on the soles of the feet and guide it through the lower navel, the kidneys, then lead it up the spine to the crown of the head, called the *baihui* point, down through the *renzhong*, and so forth. In this way, single-mindedly place your focus on circulating the *qi* around the micro- and macrocosmic orbits. However, in the fall and through the winter, it is more appropriate to post indoors. Also, one should not allow the soles of one's feet to be in contact with the floor so as to avoid absorbing 'cold' *qi* [from the floor].

"It is best to wear loose clothes when posting, the less constraining the better. According to people's different bodily constitutions, there may be varying outcomes due to the movement of *qi*, but focus the mind on all changes happening in the body, and do not respond impulsively to any of its urges. When the *qi* begins to move, collect your attention and place it on the *tanzhong* point at the center of the chest and the area of the lower *dantian*. Alternating attention between these two points, adjust the breath. This will draw the attention away from the movement of *qi*. If the mind starts to wander or becomes chaotic, adjust the position of the feet by turning them slightly in and imagining a hexagram on the soles. Slowly, the mind will become focused. If the mind becomes impatient or if anger flares, practice the 'Bound Horse Stance': Bend the knees more deeply, allowing them to pass over the toes. Do this until the breathing becomes more coarse—to the point of becoming audible—and then return to the original position.

"If you feel like your arms and hands are sore, numb, itchy, painful, or swollen, you must visualize that two fish full of life and vigor, one red and one white, appear in the formless taiji ball that you are holding between your arms and chest. At first, they slowly and unhurriedly go around the taiji clockwise, one to ten times, and then the same thing counter-clockwise. As you do this, your whole body should be relaxed, from skin to marrow. Your spine should be erect like an iron column. Between each of the 33 vertebrae, from the lower spine (coccygeal vertebrae) all the way up to those in the neck (cervical vertebrae), visualise intangible, formless, weightless crystal balls set on each intervertebral disk and propping the next one up. When your practice reaches great depth, you will be able to feel these oscillating. This will be beneficial to all those suffering from spurs, osteoporosis, scoliosis, and like conditions. Many people who suffered from discomfort in the arms or legs and those with reflexive conditions stemming from pathological changes around the spinal cord have seen improvements through the practice of posting."

Concerning the human spine—whether it's the cervical column starting at the back of the head, or the thoracic column to which the nerves of the ribs and lower trunk connect, the lumbar column nerves which provide for the legs, or the nerves of the sacrum which support the soles of the feet, the calves and the thighs—it is generally overlooked that the spinal cord is the overall link between the brain and very important segments of the central nervous system, as well as the reflex center of all five viscera and six bowels. This cord of around 50 centimeters comprises all sensory and motor nerves, and all aspects of human sensory perception, whether internal or external or the autonomic nervous system. Also, all feelings of temperature, pain, and reflex occasioned by jolts or shakes will, according to their magnitude, directly penetrate to a very deep level, even affecting the body on a cellular level. In summary, all the areas involved in the practice of posting have a direct influence on the human body. It follows naturally that, if one posts accordingly, the benefits reaped will far surpass the effects of any medicine one could ingest.

CHAPTER **63**

IMPARTING INSTRUCTION AND DISPELLING DOUBTS WITHOUT HOLDING ANYTHING BACK

Sifu also told us that when you reach a deeper stage in your posting practice, it is possible to incorporate the "Dragon Horse Bearing the Diagram Mind Practice" to the posture. Upon inhalation, crouch slightly; on exhalation, turn the palms down and extend the arms while slowly straightening the body. Upon the next inhalation, turn the arms and the palms up while crouching again. Repeat this a total of 64 times, matching the movements with the inhalations and exhalations.

Sifu told us that this movement is not only good for the circulation of blood and *qi*, but also quickens the movement of *qi* around the micro- and macrocosmic orbits and ensures the *qi* does not get stuck anywhere in the body. This combination of seated and moving practice will, in time, give rise to great capacity. *Sifu* further said that when he feels somewhat tired, or slightly uncomfortable in a particular area, or perhaps when his *qi* is not circulating to a particular point, he needs only to practice this method of combining the breath and the movement of *qi* to get immediate results. For this reason, *sifu* has maintained this practice with unwavering regularity.

At this time, *sifu* unexpectedly shared insights that he had obtained from years of posting practice with us. This was truly a great gift. After practicing with these tips for two or three years, many of the students improved various chronic problems that had been bothering them. By circulating the *qi* around the micro- and macrocosmic orbits through intention, their *qi* and blood (circulation) naturally opened up. Some reported to *sifu* that their kidneys often felt numb and hot, to the point where the revolving inner *qi* impacted their reproductive organ. *Sifu* assured them that this was only the changes that occurred in the physical body during the initial stages of practice and that they needn't pay any attention to it. Prior to the true *yang* being unleashed, these are just natural responses of the body while waiting for the spirit to guide the *qi*, for the *yin* and *yang* to meld as one, triggering the true *qi* and spirit to come together. To proceed from there to a state of luminous and void spirit, one needs the guidance of a knowledgeable master and furthermore one's own diligent practice is of utmost importance.

For more than a decade I followed *sifu*, from the time of being yet confused and uninitiated, all the way through circulating the micro- and macrocosmic orbits and up to "orienting the five vital breaths to the origin" and "transforming essence and *qi* to spirit." During that time, *sifu* meticulously revealed to me all sorts of practice methods, and even the oral tips of various sects, without concealing the slightest thing. It was like the contents of a vessel being poured out. This openness, warmth, and bearing is something virtually beyond the reach of modern people. I personally feel that the rare opportunity to follow a teacher and acquire precious teachings from them is the greatest endowment of a fully endowed human life. The treasures of instruction that *sifu* passed on to me are truly too abundant to be related in these few pages. All I can do is silently wait on those with a connection, and give out pieces when the time is ripe.

Practice Appendix

This appendix contains the essential points of the earlier chapters of the book and is intended to be a practical guide to the exercises – with detailed illustrations and step-by-step instruction.

MEDITATION

If you want to cleanse yourself, the only way is to empty out all of your contents until you are an empty cup. In the same way, stillness in meditation must start with emptying out the mind.

BASIC MEDITATION TECHNIQUE

FULL LOTUS

1. Whether you are in full or half lotus, sitting cross-legged or on a chair with feet touching the ground, you need only concern yourself with keeping your legs in the most comfortable position possible. Relax your whole body, especially the muscles. If the muscles are taut, it is very hard for the mind to become still.

2. Beginners in meditation are advised to place a 3–5 centimeters thick cushion under their buttocks, which will allow them to sit for longer periods of time and collect the body and mind. Decide on the cushion's size according to the proportions of your own body, but it cannot be too soft, nor can it be filled with a sponge base or it will impede circulation and the *qi* won't pass through. The ideal material is coconut fibers wrapped in cloth—it is of just the right firmness, won't cause any skin problems, and will allow the *qi* and air to circulate.

HALF LOTUS

3. Use your intention to simultaneously straighten and lengthen your torso, waist, and spine. Be careful not to use too much force or your fire *qi* will easily rise.

4. The abdomen and *dantian* should be drawn back without slouching.

5. The anus should be slightly contracted, but not forcefully because this could result in excessive heat in the body, as well as hemorrhoids.

6. Place the hands in the *samadhi mudra*. This means the hands are placed in the lap, below the *dantian*, with the palms facing upward. One hand is laid above the other with the thumbs gently touching. For men, the left hand should be on top; for women, the right. This position will help the circulation of blood and *qi*, keeping them unobstructed for the duration of the practice. This posture is very much like creating a connection to unite and harmonize the polarities of *yin* and *yang*, as in the taiji.

CROSS-LEGGED

7. The chest should be slightly concave, but kept relaxed and open. This will allow the breathing to be smooth and unhindered, the idea being that the breath should be able to move freely.

8. Keep the shoulders even without teetering to one side or swaying to and fro. Free of force or tension, let them relax and settle at the sides.

9. Let the head sit forward at about a 15-degree angle while tucking in the chin. The purpose of this motion is to apply pressure to the two arteries in the neck. Our brains can get tangled up in thoughts—thoughts that are largely dictated by these two arteries. Applying slight pressure to them can harmonize the spirit and mind.

10. The eyes are half closed, half open. This position, called "draping the veil," suggests that we naturally let the eyes droop without closing them completely. As to your gaze, let it peer through ever so slightly without opening the eyes wide. Eyes wide open can be overstimulating and make it hard to focus. Conversely, with closed eyes it is easy to feel drowsy and muddle-headed.

11. Now find a point on which to lightly fix your gaze. This point, about a fist's length from the tip of the nose, should be imagined as a small, transparent, formless sphere. Resting your line of sight on this sphere will focus your mind and spirit and prevent your awareness from "straying outward." Coupled with the right breathing, this constitutes the whole of the exercise.

12. The tongue is slightly curled back, with the tip pressing against the upper palate.

13. The head should be straight and the chin tucked in slightly. A smile will relax the nerves of the face.

Pre-Meditation Warmup

1. Before meditating, first stretch out your arms and legs, massage your joints and acupoints, rotate your head and your eyes around in their sockets, tuck the chin in slightly and bring the head back a number of times.

2. Move the head to the left and right toward the shoulders.

3. Rotate the head and neck clockwise and counterclockwise a few times.

4. Rotate the shoulders and arms by swinging the arms from left to right.

5. Bring the hands together and bend forward at the waist as you try to touch the ground.

6. Place the hands on the hips and twist the torso to the left and to the right.

7. Repeatedly rotate your hips in a full circle clockwise and counterclockwise.

8. Lightly pat and rub the inner and outer thighs and calves.

9. Form loose fists and pat the buttocks.

10. Make circles with your knees by placing your hands on the kneecaps.

11. Rotate the ankles, one foot at a time.

12. Squat down and stand up a few times.

13. Finish by marching in place until the breath becomes even again.

EXERCISE TO PURGE THE IMPURE AND ABSORB THE PURE

When you are about to sit, if you feel mentally or physically fatigued, sluggish or groggy, don't rush into your meditation. First you must "purge the impure and absorb the pure" with this simple exercise.

1. Use both hands to gently pat and rub the chest, the lower back, and the four limbs.

2. Breathing in through the nose, use your intention to draw the breath down to the *dantian*. On the out-breath, simultaneously

exhale through the mouth with a "Ha" sound while thrusting the body forward from the waist up like a horse bobbing its head. Do this three times. After this exercise, you will feel that your energy has been stirred and any murky heaviness will dissipate.

EXERCISES FOR EXITING MEDITATION

1. Join the soles of the feet and rub them together until hot.

2. Pat and rub the thighs from inside to out. Repeat a few times.

3. Stand up and make circles with your knees by placing your hands on the kneecaps.

4. Placing your hands on your hips, repeatedly rotate clockwise and counterclockwise.

5. Wrap up the exercise by simply marching in place.

TIPS ON BREATHING

– Start your meditation by counting the breath from 1 to 10, then from 10 back down to 1. There's no need to force or control the breath, so just breathe naturally. While counting, try to place your attention on the rise and fall of the breath, and never attempt to suppress or do away with your thoughts. Just go with whatever is natural lest you stoke the body's fire *qi*.

– Whenever your body feels heavy and weak or you feel dispirited, place your focus on the air you take in through your in-breaths.

– Whenever you feel overstimulated, or your mind is buzzing with scattered thoughts, or you feel like a heat wave is moving through your body, focus on the air as it is expelled through your out-breaths.

- What Zhuang Zi really meant when he said "The true man breathes from the heels" was that through practicing meditation, through regulating one's breath, by degrees, one's breath will become deeper and more settled. The stage where breath becomes soundless is not, however, a matter of reaching the heels in one gulp.

- When newborn babies breathe, they make fists with both hands and place them on the belly as it rises and falls. This is a great secret.

- When the breathing moves to a deeper level, it will become more like that of a turtle. Finally, you will attain turtle breathing, which means that you have practiced to the point where your acquired breathing pattern has transformed back into your original prenatal breathing pattern.

TIPS ON CULTIVATING THE MIND

- Stopping or controlling scattered thoughts is as difficult as trying to stop a torrent of water that has fallen 1,000 meters over a cliff's edge. If you persist in this method, it may become an obsession, which in itself becomes an illness. The words "Let everything be natural; forego all clinging; let go of all your connections to this world; leave only the original breath," are just a reference to the mind.

- The mind's natural state is stillness. Only in a state of stillness is the mind able to penetrate the frivolousness of worldly desires such as fame, wealth, and romance. During meditation practice, many people attempt to focus the mind on controlling their thoughts. However, this is like pouring gasoline on a bonfire; instead of calming the mind, it actually creates more distracting thoughts.

- You can't just use force or sheer willpower to tell your mind to stop thinking. Its transformation must start from the very root—desire and attachment.

- Have you ever noticed when you are not meditating that your mind is free of distracted thought? Yet whenever you want to sit and become still, you feel as if your head is suddenly filled with the relentless stampede of 1,000 galloping horses. The principle behind this is akin to shaking a glass of water and setting it on a table in the sun. You would be able to see many little objects floating about. This is what happens to the mind when we meditate.

- If you want to make your mind tranquil, you have to empty the glass. When you want to become still during meditation, first you must empty the mind.

- If the mind is scattered, the spirit will be muddled. If the mind is empty, the spirit will be clear. If the mind is occupied, desires will be many. If the mind is unoccupied, it will be clear and empty. If you want to meditate, you should therefore first empty your mind and clear away desire. You can try reciting the *Heart Sutra* one to three times before starting your session.

- When practicing meditation, you mustn't strain yourself. Your body and mind should both be relaxed. Your mental state should be free-flowing and natural. When thoughts arise, just let them come; and if they stay, just let them stay. You are the host and your thoughts are merely guests. They come and go of their own accord and there is no need to follow them or to get involved in their affairs. This is how you begin to relax.

- People of today, even from childhood, are overrun by an onslaught of wild and fantastic thoughts. It has already become a habit and is very difficult to stop. Once we sit in meditation, and the body and senses no longer divert our attention, the myriad delusive thoughts grow like wildfire. According to the Daoist perspective, this is the rising of fire within the body.

The lower body naturally becomes deficient and weak in the meditation posture, and circulation becomes obstructed.

- If someone is heavy or brooding with thoughts as they sit, their face will flush. Be very careful with this, for many will mistake rosy cheeks as a good sign, but this is actually just an accumulation of blood in the brain. In serious cases this will cause tinnitus, stuffiness in the head, dizziness, headaches, and bloodshot eyes. This means that the elements of water and fire in the body are totally out of balance. That's why it's important to remind yourself to discard all external environmental factors and maintain single-mindedness during meditation.

- Excessive thinking will harm the kidney *qi*, and when the kidney *qi* becomes weak, the lower back and knees will easily become weak and shaky, making it impossible to continue with seated meditation. You need to first start by refining your physical temperament. What exactly does this mean? It means to train one's mind to cultivate one's physical condition. If your body is not settled, the posture will not be correct. If the posture is not proper, then *qi* will not be achieved and the spirit cannot maintain oneness and peacefulness. How does one concentrate the spirit until it becomes supple? The most important thing is to start from having no desire. Before sitting for meditation, you must empty your mind. Only an empty mind can be clear and bright, and when the mind is bright, your body will be centered and still. This is one of the important oral tips when practicing the physical aspect of the alchemical principle of body and mind.

- Within the *Yi Jing* it says: "Inquire after ultimate truth and bring out the best of a person's self-nature, to the end that both are integrated into a person's life." Reaching the "oneness of heaven and humanity" during meditation, however, depends entirely on the training and disciplining of the mind. If you sit there like a stagnant pool of water, you will definitely miss the true power of meditation, and it will be of no benefit whatsoever to your health.

- In the deepest states of stillness, the meditator would not so much as bat an eyelid if a swarm of flies buzzed past their ears. Even if 1,000 ants were to crawl over their body they would remain unmoved, their mind as vast as the galaxies and free from any disturbance.

- As a matter of fact, when it comes to studying the Dao, the most important part is having a mind that is relaxed, quiet, complete, and stable. The mind in a state of true rest is like a wild goose gliding silently over a pool, or like a boat drifting over a river, leaving no lines upon the water. Whether speaking, silent, moving, or still, the mind is at rest and peaceful. When a meditator's mind becomes truly still, they become like a person engulfed in a teeming crowd; paying no attention to the turmoil of the mortal world, they stay untainted. It makes no difference whether they are moving or still. This is a state that can only be entered into when fully relaxed.

- In the deepest states of stillness the mind abides in a singular, uniform stillness, otherwise known in Buddhism as the state of "suchness." The utmost pinnacle of this state can be described as the emptiness of both the mind and the state itself. In the beginning stages of practice this state is attainable through sitting meditation. As you gradually deepen your practice of this state, you can reach the point where even subtle discursive thoughts do not arise as you go about various activities in your day, whether conversing, driving, eating, using the toilet, or even while sleeping.

- True "completeness" surpasses even the state of *xin zhai zuo wang* in that you go beyond just "forgetting" reputation, fortune, food, sleep, praise, criticism, success, and failure. Through the practice of the mind and maintaining stillness, you reach a level where you are immersed in the material world yet remain unmoved by what the eyes see, the ears hear, the nose smells, the tongue tastes, the body touches, and the mind thinks. It is a state where your six roots and six governing dusts no longer serve as obstructions. Notions such as "self and other," or "right and wrong" are completely powerless to disturb the mind. The mind is broad, open, clear, illuminated, and boundless. This is the ultimate relaxation, stillness, perfection, and settling, and it is only possible when one's meditation occurs seamlessly whether in motion or at rest. Only if you meditate to this level will you truly experience the complete transformation of yourself.

– At times, when entering deeper meditative stillness, you might experience a sudden surge of brightness that illuminates the mind, akin to the borderless sky that encompasses all happenings yet remains unfettered nevertheless. Don't feel complacent when joyous occasions occur; likewise, your mind should not yield to the upheaval brought about by calamities. It is much the same as this: though we may change clothes daily, the fabric is always wrapped around the same odorous sac of red flesh and bones.

ESSENTIAL TIPS FOR MEDITATION

– A sharp practitioner will always be ready to grab any opportunity to practice, whenever or wherever it presents itself. When still, sit in meditation; when in movement, practice the mind.

– True meditation takes place in the midst of the most clamorous situations, when the meditator maintains calm without giving rise to anger. In a noisy marketplace, they are like a pure and serene maiden. The merits of achieving this are superior to 1,000 meditation sessions.

– The great Dao is uncomplicated and none other than a wondrous emptiness. In your leisure time, regulate your breath and collect your *shen* (spirit) and *qi* in the area just below your navel. Count your breaths as they come in and out until they number into the thousands. If you are able to remain calm during the counting then collect the "six gates," you will slowly come to the point where you feel the whole world around you and it seems that the whole world around you, including your breath, comes to a stop. In this state, it's like the way a cat keeps a watchful eye on the mouse. No need to forcefully pursue—just knowing is enough. Gradually, a surge of *yang qi* will naturally emerge of itself.

- The key to meditation is to be at peace wherever you go and maintain a tranquil mind at all times. The breath should consistently be smooth and even, with your awareness on both the inhalation and exhalation allowing you to regularly enter a state of extreme stillness. This kind of utmost quiescence is in actual fact the primary divinity (original spirit) and the original *qi* (referring to the mind) according to Daoist terminology. However, all Daoist schools of thought simply refer to this as having "opened the gate of the taiji (the ultimate or absolute). The so-called "true seed" is the original *qi* stemming from the void. If a practitioner is able to grasp the opportunity while they get hold of the "true seed" to turn the celestial chariot, what they could achieve is indeed invaluable. This is considered the ultimate attainment for all Daoist practitioners.

- Many Daoist practitioners quite enjoy the state of "emptiness" through their meditation practice. This in fact requires great caution. No matter how placid your meditation allows you to become, retain a watchful awareness within your primary divinity (original spirit); otherwise you will not reach a high state. In the end, one will reside continuously in the truth with the brightness of alert and knowing awareness. This is where the "true medicine" dwells and is also the true way to "collect the pill." No matter how high your meditative state seems to be, this is the method to preserve it, like a dragon guarding its pearls.

EXERCISES

Arm Swinging

Practicing this Arm Swinging *qigong* can help to protect the kidney *qi*, as well as unblock the pathways for the *qi* and blood to move. If used along with meditation, this practice can lead to the opening of the micro- and macrocosmic orbits.

1. Before swinging your arms, stand with feet shoulder-width apart. Wear no socks or shoes, preferably standing on the grass so your feet can absorb the essence from the earth. Begin visualizing, from the top of your head all the way down to the soles of your feet, that your body is slowly loosening up like a deflating balloon. Repeat this three times.

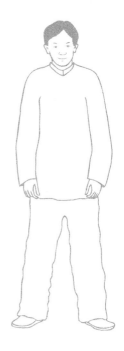

2. Now regulate your breath by inhaling slowly until the *qi* settles into the *dantian*, then exhale through the nose three times.

3. Next, bring awareness to the lower abdomen and completely relax this area. Avoid holding your breath; just gently keep your awareness in the lower abdomen about 4 fingers' width below the belly button.

4. While performing the arm swinging, keep your arms straight and your palms flat. The muscles and even the skeletal structure must be completely relaxed, without exerting unnecessary force. In the beginning stage, just make sure your mind, muscles, and joints are all summarized by a single word: "relaxed."

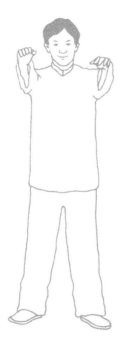

5. Now swing your arms back with about 70 percent of your force, and allow them to bounce back with about 30 percent of your remaining force.

6. Gently grasp the earth with your toes when the arms swing backward. This will enhance blood and *qi* circulation and stimulate bowel movement. You should notice some perspiration and warmth in your stomach—signs of good blood and *qi* circulation.

7. The eyes should look straight ahead to a distant point, with a relaxed gaze. Try to use your intention instead of force while doing this. When the aforementioned symptoms arise, you may close your eyes, yet still maintain your gaze toward a distant point in front of you. Doing this can help collect the spirit, *qi*, and essence in one place.

FOCUS POINTS

– As much as is possible, you should keep your mind in a state that is unsusceptible to external influence when doing the Arm Swinging exercise. The reason is that the circulation of *qi* and blood is easily stagnated by excessive thinking and worry. In addition, clots can form when the mind is scattered and unable to focus.

– Frantic mental activity easily ignites a vacuous heat to rise in the body, which at a certain point will cause ringing in the ears and sensitivity in the teeth. If not dealt with soon enough, eventually the skin will break out in rashes. When it gets to this point, you need to take a timeout and regulate your breathing. Allow the breath to become natural and even, keep silent, and draw your vision and hearing inward. Gently place your focus on the breath. You can sit or stand, but you are centered on reining in all of the thoughts flying around in your head. When you feel your focus has returned to normal, you can continue with the Arm Swinging exercise. Before you have deepened your practice of observing the acupoints, it's not necessary to place your focus on any one point; rather just focus on the natural inhalations and exhalations of your breath.

POSTING (HORSE STANCE)

Beginners of meditation practice can first practice the Horse Stance to help open the meridians and support the three treasures of the body: essence, energy, and spirit. This standing meditation practice will help improve your sitting meditation practice.

Beginners who sit for an extended period of time may suffer from stagnant *qi* below the waist. Posting at this stage can supplement their meditation by regulating the flow of *qi*, and complementing the essence and spirit. Based on the principles of moving and stillness, *yin* and *yang*, ancient sages created these exercises to complement their meditation practice. Furthermore, those who sit for long hours at an office job can, every couple of hours or so, stand up and do a round of posting practice. This will help keep the body's *qi* and blood moving smoothly while at the same time prevent excess blood from accumulating in the upper portion of the body, especially the brain.

1. To start, walk in place as if you are taking a leisurely walk. This helps regulate your mind and breath. Do this until the breath

is fine and long and you have brought your body under greater control.

2. Once this is achieved, and your body and mind are both relaxed, feel as though your breath, fine and gentle, is the only thing that exists in the world at this moment. From the space above you a fine drizzle falls onto your hair, then enters and washes your body, purifying it with the five vital elements, namely: earth, water, fire, air, and space. The rain falls onto the skin, penetrating the dermis and subcutaneous tissues and gradually reaching the fasciae and muscle. The rain further purifies all the nerve cells, revitalizing the withering, aging, and broken cells. It also purifies all internal organs, including the heart, brain, spleen, kidneys, lungs, stomach, and spine. You should feel your spirit invigorated and renewed after this visualization.

3. Then stand with feet shoulder-width apart, and relax the whole body. When the body is relaxed through and through, bend the knees slightly, as if they are gently pulled down by gravity. Make sure your knees don't extend past the toes.

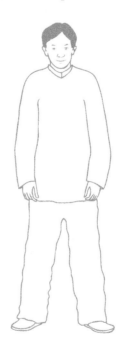

4. Gently bring your awareness to the *yongquan* acupoint at the soles of both feet. Relax, and while you are fully relaxed you will feel a surge of warmth bubbling up through the *yongquan* point and rising rapidly to the lower *dantian*, the waist area between the kidneys.

5. With the rise of the warm current, the arms rise simultaneously, forming a circle as if holding a tree. The fingers of each hand face each other with about a fist's distance separating the two. The hands naturally stay in this even position, with the palms facing toward the body. Visualize that your arms are embracing a formless taiji.

6. Slightly tuck in the chin, and keep the eyes half open, half closed, with the gaze fixed on a point about a meter ahead.

7. Relax once more and adjust your breathing, counting your breaths first from 1 to 10, then backward from 10 to 1. Inhale and exhale from the nose. On the inhale the tongue rolls up and presses against the upper palate, and on the exhale it rolls down and presses the lower palate. Here, focus your attention on the

lower *dantian*. Visualize that everything you hear is melding with the *dantian*. With each out-breath, visualize all the illness and worries expelled from the body into the space around.

8. Next, visualize the body emptying layer by layer, both inside and outside. If the concept of emptiness eludes you, you may simply allow your focused attention to provide the impetus to relax from the skin, working your way in until the only thing left is the mind.

QI PIAN QUAN SHEN

This method of *qigong* is suitable to add at the end of another *qigong* practice. Its effects are most felt when you use it as such a concluding exercise.

1. Your legs should be of equal width as your shoulders. Naturally allow the hands to come up to chest height with the palms of both hands facing downward.

2. With your hands in front of the chest, gradually have the hands move downward until they are level with the waist. Then, you need to slowly crouch down as you continue to move downward.

3. When the hands get to the ground, keep them even as they raise up and as your body raises up from crouching. The body and the hands raise together and the hands raise up all the way to above the head. The hands come down to the starting position and continue down to a place between the front of the chest and the *dantian*. Slowly come to a stop and position your hands as if you are a holding a ball.

4. The area below the waist remains still as the area above the waist rotates to the left and then returns to the center.

5. Following that, the body (above the waist) rotates to the right and then returns once again to the center.

6. Lift the left leg and, in a relaxed manner, kick it out to the left. Lift the right leg up and then kick it out to the right.

7. Finally, have the hands return and move to the side of the thighs.

DRAGON HORSE PRACTICE

When you have reached a higher level in your posting practice, you can incorporate the Dragon Horse Practice into the original posture.

1. Gradually bend at the knees on the in-breath.

2. On the out-breath, start by flipping the palms over to face the floor. Gradually extend the arms outward while slowly rising up and straightening the body from a slight crouch.

3. Inhaling, flip the palms toward the sky while retracting the arms and slowly returning to a crouching position.

4. Repeat this set 64 times, aligning each movement with the in-and-out breaths.

BACKSTEPPING PEACOCK

This exercise can strengthen less commonly used muscle groups, as well as aid in weight loss. The extension of the spine as instructed is also of general benefit to spinal health.

1. Interlace the fingers with the exception of the middle fingers. The middle fingers should be fully extended and pressed together, and the hands clasped tightly.

2. Raise your clasped hands over your head and straighten the arms, while also simultaneously bringing the heels off the ground until you are standing on the tips of your toes. Imagine an energy originating from the crown of your head and spreading upward. The whole body should now be in full extension.

3. From this position, begin walking backward on the balls of your feet. Continue until you are short of breath, and rest. Try to increase the number of steps you can take with each session, doing so at a pace that is comfortable for you.

4. You can get even better results if you practice this exercise on a slope or inclined surface.

IMMORTAL SITTING QIGONG (SQUATTING QIGONG)

This *qigong* is beneficial for improving curvature in the spine, bone spurs and other spine-related issues. It also improves the waist and kidney functioning and strength. This *qigong* can be beneficial for both men and women.

1. Begin with the legs wider than shoulder width and then place the spine and back close up to a wall. Relax your entire body, from the head down to the feet, and allow your breathing to be natural and even.

2. Adjust your breath to the point of it becoming smooth and unhindered. After your entire body is relaxed, allow your body to slowly squat down. While squatting, make sure that your back and spine remain close up to the wall. During the squat, the feet need to be pointed out slightly in the shape of a "V."

3. Squat down until the buttocks and knees are at the same level, as if you are riding a horse.

4. To finish, slowly raise yourself back up to the original position.

CLAPPING PRACTICE

The fingers and the palms of the hand are connected to the five organs and six viscera. This *qigong* method can stimulate the acupoints of the fingers and hands. It is also effective in maintaining the health of the five organs.

1. Bring the hands up in front of the chest, with the palms facing inward and facing each other. Begin to tap the fingers together: thumb to thumb, pointer finger to pointer finger, middle finger to middle finger, ring finger to ring finger, pinky to pinky. This

tapping will stimulate the acupoints of the fingers. Do this a total of 28 times.

2. After you have stimulated the fingers, clasp your hands together with the fingers crossed and the palms facing inward. The space between each finger must match up with its corresponding space on the other hand. Unclasp and clasp your hands together, so as to tap the interdigital folds (the skin between the fingers) against those of the other hand. Do this 28 times.

3. Next, raise the hands evenly, palms facing upward. Keep the hands and fingers straight, like a blade, and tap together the outer edges of the palms (the side of the pinkies). Do this 28 times.

4. Following this, tap the bottom of the wrists together 28 times in total.

5. Afterward, tap the edge of the palm area, on the thumb side, together a total of 28 times.

6. Finally, tap the back of the hands together for a total of 28 times.

7. Now, bring the hands up to the sides of the body, with the palms facing outward, and stretch the arms out.

8. Using the palms, use force to clap the hands together. This exercise has no limit to the number of times that you can do it. You need to do it until the palms of the hands are a bit numb and painful; only then will it be effective.

9. This exercise can be used in conjunction with a walking method. While you are standing on an inclined surface, practice walking backward up the incline. If you add this part in, the qigong will be even more effective. You must use more of your strength to walk this way. Also, walking backward has another added benefit: it allows you to use muscles that you normally don't use.

THE SLEEPING POSTURE OF THE SCHOOL OF COMPLETE REALITY

This sleeping method is easy, but potent. Once you start using it, you will gradually find it easier to fall asleep naturally. In addition, it will dramatically improve the quality of your sleep.

1. Before you sleep, you must remember to rest your mind before closing your eyes. Your breath should be calm and even, your hands should rest naturally at your sides, your legs should lie straight and your toes should be pointing up toward the sky.

2. Breathe through your nostrils. When you exhale, move your toes forward toward the ground. When you inhale, bring your toes back to their resting position. If your mind and body are relaxed and you just follow your breath with the movements, sleep will come naturally.

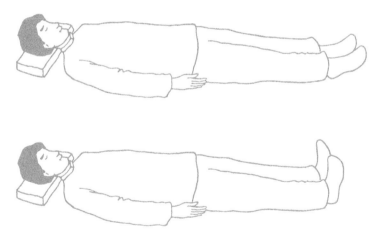

MEDITATION Q&A

Q: I began practicing recently and cannot do a double lotus position. Even a half lotus I can barely hold for five minutes. Can I practice meditation like this?

A: Yes, of course! Just use whatever posture is most comfortable for you. Start your meditation by counting the breath from 1 to 10, then from 10 back down to 1. There's no need to force or control the breath, so just breathe naturally. While counting, try to place your attention on the rise and fall of the breath, and never attempt to suppress or do away with your thoughts. Just go with whatever is natural lest you stoke the body's fire *qi*.

Q: When meditating, what is the importance of having your thumbs lightly touching each other? Does it really matter where you put your hands?

A: This action can help keep your mind in one place. It's known as "Ten Fingers Open the Heart," and the finger of special significance is the thumb. People's fingertips connect to their internal organs. The thumb correlates to the cerebrum, so the touching of the thumbs creates balance and can also help to stop discursive thoughts. Additionally, massaging the fingers is an excellent daily health care method. People should massage their thumbs more often, thereby also preserving the health of their cerebrum. The index finger connects to our intestines and stomach; the middle finger directly to the heart; the ring finger can support the liver; and the little finger supports the kidneys.

If you can understand the fundamental concepts of health preservation, when acute illnesses suddenly arise you can have an influence on them. If discomfort, gas, bloating, or loose bowel movements originate in the visceral organs, stomach, or intestines, you can simply massage your index fingers. For the heart, for an oppressive and constrictive feeling in the chest, or a tight pain, you can massage the middle fingers and thumbs. If the heart and lung function are not good, or if you have a weak respiratory system, you can often massage the ring fingers. Likewise, if the kidney organ is not healthy, resulting in a sore, painful back and waist, or poor circulation of the *qi* and blood, you can often massage the little finger.

Q: When doing seated meditation, is sitting for longer better?

A: Many people ask about lengthening the period of time they are able to sit in the lotus posture. Such concerns shouldn't be given too much time. We all have a limited number of years to spend in this world. Don't spend it on questions like this. I've seen people squander a lifetime working on the condition of their legs. By the time the *qi* and blood are unobstructed and the capacity to maintain full lotus for a period of time is available, it is nearly time to move on to the next world. This is not a good use of time. We can't compete with trees, rocks, tables, or chairs. What do they get from 100 or even 1,000 years of sitting still? This way, there will be no chance to attain enlightenment, to develop wisdom, or to practice the combined cultivation of body and mind.

For those more advanced in years, I advise sitting on a wooden bench. It will be enough if the feet can make contact with the *qi* of the earth. Another method is to sit on raised cushions, high enough to avoid pain, numbness, or other discomfort in the legs. In the beginning, when setting a foundation for meditation practice, sit in a natural, cross-legged position, relax the entire body and keep the eyes half open. Set the eyes on any point 3–5 meters ahead without straining. Over-exertion may cause the eyes to feel swollen. This may even create the false impression that the eyes have developed a sort of supernatural power. Most importantly, keep the mind relaxed; and if it wanders, bring it back. At first, there is no need to put focus on any specific point. Whatever experiences come, disregard them.

Q: If I often feel muddled, is it best if I close my eyes during meditation?

A: During meditation, you should keep the eyes somewhere halfway between closed and open. There is a phrase that describes this position, "draping the curtains," a way to illustrate the natural position into which the eyelids fall if lowered without closing completely. As the eyes are very literally the windows to the soul (and the mind), you cannot wholly close off the spirit. As soon as you do, you'll actually find yourself having more thoughts. The only time you should give your eyes a rest is when your mind is overactive. Even out the breath and refresh your spirit before continuing. The best way to give yourself a daily outlet is to collect the mind and spirit, with eyes half open and half closed.

Q: Why is it necessary to tuck in the chin during meditation? Doesn't it make our breathing smoother if we straighten the neck?

A: Following the correct posture for meditation, the head should be tilted slightly forward at about 15 degrees, with the chin slightly tucked. Actually, the desired effect here is a slight compression of the two arteries running through the neck. These two arteries are largely responsible for all of the thoughts that are constantly flooding our brain. Compressing the arteries therefore has the effect of settling the mind and spirit.

Q: There are times during meditation that my mind feels restless and frenetic. It's hard to stay seated when I feel like this. What can I do to help my mind in this situation?

A: In situations like this where you feel restless and antsy, as if there's something important about to happen, or you feel anxious and tightness in the chest, this all points to excessive fire in the heart. As an antidote to this, you can use the practice of focusing on the acupoints. In a very relaxed manner, place your focus on the *shanggen* acupoint (located on the bridge of the nose between the eyes. Hold your focus there for 3–7 breaths before moving your focus down to the point 4½ fingers' width below the naval (the *dantian*). Gradually your chest and mind will loosen up and become calm.

If you notice that your mind begins to drift after sitting for a while, you may gently close the eyes and bring your awareness to the *dantian*. Breathe naturally, and when your mind and spirit are focused again, open your eyes and retain their half-open and half-closed state. If you feel heavy, drowsy and unable to focus on any acupoint, clench your hands into fists with the thumbs pressed against the root of the ring fingers, then place the fists facing downward on your inner thighs near the groin and stretch the arms, staring straight ahead with eyes wide open. Repeat this a few times until any remaining drowsiness is cleared. If the mind is filled with frivolous, negative, or even obsessive thoughts, simply watch these thoughts for a while. Visualize them exiting with each exhalation and congealing into a spot about a fist's distance in front of the tip of the nose. Continue doing so until the mind is calm, then resume your meditation.

Q: Is there a particular time of the day that's ideal for meditating?

A: In meditation and the regulation of one's breath, one must also understand the *zi* period (from 11pm to 1am) and the *wu* period (from 11am to 1pm) as well as other optimal times for the flow of certain channels. The human breath is divided into flourishing, assisted, dead, resting, and imprisoned. The period before noon is prime time to develop your *qi* through meditation, though the absolute best times are during the *zi* and *wu* periods. It is best if the methods and times for meditative practice can be transmitted to you via an experienced teacher.

Q: I work in sales as a manager and have to deal with sales targets and manage the team to achieve them. I'm guessing that this is why I've been feeling overstressed and, consequently, am having trouble sleeping. My mind feels especially frenetic and unfocused when I meditate, and my chest feels heavy like there's something there that I can't release. These meditation sessions are not very effective. Is there something I can do about this?

A: There are numerous reasons for losing sleep. It's known in Traditional Chinese Medicine (TCM) as "insomnia." The elderly, people overusing the brain, those suffering from excessive phlegm in the bronchi, or those who are physically drained, agitated, and quick to anger are more likely to experience poor sleep quality. In your case, over-thinking has given you poor circulation and is drawing blood to your brain. This, in turn, makes you deficient in *qi* and agitates your mind. In TCM this is what happens when your body's water and fire elements are imbalanced. You need first and foremost to find an experienced TCM doctor who can help you restore harmony and promote your body's water and fire cycle. In advanced-level meditation, there is an oral instruction which states "The mind ends in the spine," which refers to this method.

An hour before going to bed, put all matters of business to the back of your mind. Listen to some relaxing music. Watch an entertaining television show. Do some light reading. You can soak your feet in a basin of hot salt water for about 15–30 minutes, which helps draw blood downward into your feet. After soaking, use your fingers to massage, or your fist to gently pat, the spot in the middle of your heel. This should be done gently and without causing discomfort.

Q: I have cardiovascular disease. Can sitting meditation help?

A: Just as Patriarch Lu Chun Yang said: "When you sit for meditation, you need only to expel all distracting thoughts and desires and purify your mind. Your mind and breath will eventually join seamlessly and you will come to feel light and full of energy and vitality. If you can sustain these practices, it will have the effect of naturally regulating and balancing the organs and viscera."

These techniques also conform to the principles explained in the *Yellow Emperor's Internal Classic*. They are particularly apt when dealing with chronic problems related to the blood vessels connected to the heart. If you are able to temporarily stop all frivolous, distracting, and delusive thoughts and relax the body and mind, the heart will be better able to regulate and aid the functions of the other organs. Furthermore, your blood will circulate more freely and your spirit will be tranquil. Supplement this by reducing your consumption of red meat, refined and oily foods, and sweets, and by adding more boiled greens, and with time your health will turn around.

Q: I have an office job and often sit for long periods. Other than sitting meditation, are there some simple exercises suitable for me?

A: Here's an exercise you can try: First, stand with your legs shoulder-width apart. Remain standing until your body is completely relaxed. Then naturally let your body sink until your legs are bent at an angle of 15 degrees. Raise your hands effortlessly until they reach chest level, keeping the fingers slightly separated with the tips pointing toward each other and about a fist's width apart. With palms facing inward, hold this posture, eyes fixed on a point in front of you. In the beginning, breathe naturally. When the entire body is completely relaxed, begin counting your breath from 1 to 10, then from 10 back to 1.

Those with high blood pressure can, after their body has completely relaxed, bring their focus to the *yongquan* point. Doing so draws the blood downward, lowering blood pressure over time. Those with a weak stomach or intestines can— again, after becoming physically relaxed—utilize a particular technique for inhalation and exhalation. This involves sucking the belly inward on the in-breath, as if you were trying to bring the breath all the way to the back. On the out-breath, relax and let the belly naturally push forward. Repeat the sequence a couple of times until you feel comfortable. This will aid bowel movement and relieve constipation. All in all, there are various techniques for posting. Every individual can benefit from the practice by finding the one best suited to their particular physical condition.

Q: I will soon be entering menopause. Will meditation be of benefit to me?

A: If you are afraid of having menopausal issues, you definitely should practice meditation to prevent aging. The conception channel is also of huge benefit to the kidney *qi*. If meditation practice is done over a long time, men will not have any problems with the prostate gland, nor will women have problems in related areas. If after meditation, the palms are rubbed together until warm, and rubbed over the *dantian* in a circular motion 64 times—clockwise for men and counterclockwise for women—no matter whether you're male or female you will reap enormous benefits. This can stabilize your foundations and nurture your original *qi*. For both men and women it can guard against the aging process, and for women this can prevent abnormal leukorrhea as well as uterine and ovarian diseases. For men it is effective in dealing with prostate problems, impotence, and deficiency of the kidneys.

Q: I often feel faint, my mind is not clear, and my body is heavy. Whenever I meditate, it is very easy for me to fall asleep. What should I do in this situation?

A: If you feel mentally or physically fatigued, sluggish or groggy, don't rush into your meditation. First you must purge the impure and absorb the pure. This involves a simple exercise using both hands to gently pat and rub the chest, the lower back, and the four limbs. Next, breathing in through the nose, use your intention to draw the breath down to the *dantian*. On the out-breath, simultaneously exhale through the mouth with a "Ha" sound while thrusting the body forward from the waist up, like a horse bobbing its head. Do this three times. After this exercise, you will feel that your energy has been stirred and any murky heaviness will dissipate.

You can regularly make use of the method I just taught you, known as the "Six Word Secret," to remove toxic *qi* from your five viscera and six bowels. During meditation, you must also be sure to properly adjust and balance the body, from the four limbs to the bones and channels. This is a simple, quick way to prevent impure *qi* from getting stuck in the body.

Q: I often hear people say that, while meditating, you must place your attention on the *dantian*. Where exactly is the *dantian*? Why is it so important?

A: The most vital life essence within our physical bodies is gathered in the area around the navel, especially in the *qihai*. The *qihai* encompasses the entire area under the navel and is one of the locations on which we should place our focus during meditation. It is the core, the control center of our body. You could compare it to the deep foundations of a skyscraper, or the frame of a towering pagoda. This is exactly why we learn to focus on the *dantian* during meditation.

Q: Sometimes when I meditate, my mouth and tongue feel dry and parched. What can I do?

A: If you feel bothered and irritated, or if you find yourself in an extremely dry climate, you can place the tip of the tongue on your palate. You will soon be able to feel calm again, and even less thirsty. Slowly swallow the saliva produced, and you will regain your physical and mental balance.

I usually combine breathing techniques with the aforementioned movement involving the tip of the tongue touching the roof of the mouth, then rolling it back and tucking in the chin. Doing so helps alleviate fatigue, and always leaves me feeling refreshed and invigorated. In Taiwan, many people experience issues with their intestinal tract and stomach. After using this method for an extended period of time, most of them found that their gastrointestinal problems miraculously vanished. In truth, it is the work of the enzymes in saliva produced during meditation.

Q: You always see the governing and conception vessels mentioned in *gongfu* novels. What exactly are these two vessels? Are they connected in any way with meditation?

A: Whether you use meditation as a means to cultivate your health or as a practice of spiritual cultivation, you will necessarily come across the conception and governing channels. From the perspective of *yin* and *yang*, the conception channel is classified as *yin* and the governing channel as *yang*. The conception channel starts at the teeth in the lower jaw and extends to the perineum. The governing channel starts at the perineum and extends to the teeth of the upper jaw. The conception channel goes downward, while the governing channel extends upward.

According to the Daoist tradition, if through the practice of austerities you "open up" these two channels, then you will have opened up the microcosmic orbit. If, beyond this, the *qixue* (*dantian*), *huangting* (around the center of the torso) and *niwan* (crown of the head) areas of the body can be opened as well, this is known as having "opened" the "macrocosmic orbit" (energy channels within the torso, head, arms, and legs).

The conception and governing channels, along with the eight extraordinary channels, are all linked. The eight extraordinary channels are composed of the conception, governing, *chong* (thoroughfare), and *dai* (girdling) channels, as well as the *yangwei* channel (*yang* linking) which governs the outer surface of the body. There is also the *yinwei* channel (*yin* linking) governing the inner section of the body, the *yangqiao* channel (*yang* springing) governing the *yang* section of the horizontal axis of the body, and the *yinqiao* channel (*yin* springing) governing the *yin* section of the horizontal axis of the body. Daoist books commonly refer to the microcosmic orbit as the movement of the celestial chariot. To put it more simply, it means the area beneath the lower lip, which in physiognomy is referred to as the *chengjiang* (sauce receptacle). From here, down to the perineum is the conception channel. Going back from the perineum, past the anus, following the sacrum, ascending to the top of the head, going down past the center of the eyebrows, tip of the nose and center of the upper lip (philtrum), before finally reaching the gums of the upper teeth, is the governing channel.

In practicing the various meditation and breathing practices of the different schools, most practitioners will experience a rise in *yang qi*. Once the vital energy of the body starts moving, this *qi* will spread and ascend, gradually making its way up the spinal column. According to various oral tips from the masters of various schools, you can drive this *qi* with the breath and in this way move it up either side of the spine to the *yuzhen* ("jade pillow" point at the back of the head), then downward from the *baihui* (crown of the head) via the *shanggen* (top of the nose), and down beyond the nostrils (*lantai*: left nostril and the *tingwei*: right nostril). The *qi* then moves past the lips to the *chengjiang* (area under the lower lip), from there it continues via the *tanzhong* (chest center) through to the stomach and intestinal area, and after one such loop it arrives at the *dantian*. Genuinely opening up the conception and governing channels is not achieved by means of intention or force. This *qi* movement arises from the practitioner being in a state of deep stillness, such that the movement of the celestial chariot happens absolutely spontaneously.

Q: What are the particular health benefits of the governing and conception vessels?

A: Opening up the conception and governing channels (the microcosmic orbit) will be of great help in dealing with most congenital or acquired deficiencies or imbalances. Endocrine imbalances and dysfunctions spring from the aging of the pituitary glands. If you can "open" your conception and governing channels through meditation practice, it will certainly change your constitution. It will directly benefit the nervous, endocrine, and hormonal systems. It can also rejuvenate you, restore youthful vigor, beautify your skin, and clear any obstructions of *qi* and blood circulation. Following a meditation session with massage can also prevent insomnia. Opening the conception and governing channels will bring an end to sensations of cold in the hands or feet, and will resolve problems of the immune system. The benefits are too many to be listed here.

Made in the USA
Las Vegas, NV
14 November 2022

59480969R00142